SUPERMARINE

SCIMITAR

SUPERMARINE

SCIMITAR

SUPERMARINE'S LAST FIGHTER

RICHARD A FRANKS

DALRYMPLE
& VERDUN

PUBLISHING

Supermarine Scimitar
Supermarine's Last Fighter
by Richard A Franks

ISBN 978-1-905414-10-9

First published in 2009 by
Dalrymple & Verdun Publishing
33 Adelaide Street
Stamford
Lincolnshire
PE9 2EN
Tel: 0845 838 1940
mail@dvpublishing.co.uk
www.dvpublishing.co.uk

Concept and design ©
Dalrymple & Verdun Publishing and
Stephen Thompson Associates
Text © Richard A Franks 2009
colour profiles © Richard J Caruana

Editor and commissioning editor
Martin Derry

Printed in England by
Ian Allan Printing Ltd
Riverdene Business Park
Molesey Road
Hersham, Surrey, KT12 4RG

Acknowledgements
I am indebted once again to Barry Jones
for all his help and assistance with this
title and for supplying many of the
images you see within it. Thanks also to
Richard J Caruana for his support, colour
artwork and scale drawings.

Publisher's acknowledgements
The publisher would like to thank the
following for their invaluable contribution.
Duncan Adams, Tony Buttler, Catherine
Cooper and Susan Dearing of the FAA
Museum, Peter Jefferies, Brian Lowe,
Chris Salter, Mike Smith Curator of the
Newark Air Museum, and Peter
Woodbridge.

CONTENTS

Half title page: Two No.736 Squadron Scimitars displaying a variation in the application of their Squadron codes. FAA Museum

Title page: HMS Victorious (R38), was the only one of six armoured fleet carriers built during World War Two to be thoroughly rebuilt and recommissioned into the post-war Royal Navy, re-entering service in 1958. Its period of service was cut short however when, following a small fire during a refit in November 1967, a government decision was taken to withdraw this vessel two years earlier than originally intended.

This photograph shows a projection attached to the bow ahead of one of the catapults and is reminiscent of a bridle catcher, although it is much smaller in appearance than those which were later fitted to Ark Royal. Brian Lowe

Opposite: HMS Ark Royal, 22nd September 1966 off Aberdeen. The ship had received Her Majesty the Queen Mother aboard and conducted an air display in her honour. A No.803 Squadron Scimitar lands on, having completed its display. FAA Museum

Chapter 1: **LAST OF THE LINE**

Just as Supermarine's Attacker held the distinction of being the first jet fighter operated by the Royal Navy, the Scimitar became the last aircraft solely designed and built by the Supermarine division of Vickers-Armstrong (Aircraft) Ltd before it became part of the British Aircraft Corporation in 1960. The development of what ultimately became the Scimitar was via a convoluted route which commenced with a requirement by the Ministry of Supply for an aircraft without undercarriage intended to be launched by a catapult accelerator and to land on a flexible deck. A flexible deck consisted of layers of thick rubber laid on a section of an aircraft carriers deck. The concept was tested both ashore at RAE Farnborough, Hampshire and afloat aboard HMS *Warrior*. Much of the radical thinking promoted during wartime still prevailed as hostilities closed which is why such an unusual requirement was under consideration. The rationale behind this was principally due to the low power outputs of jet engines at that time, so the weight saving offered by the lack of undercarriage and its associated hydraulics etc was very appealing, although the type would require some form of lightweight wheeled system to allow it to be manoeuvred on the flight deck. In February 1945, N E Rowe, Director of Technical Development (DTD) at the Ministry of Supply requested a proposal from Joe Smith at Supermarine to meet this requirement resulting in the Type 505. The powerplants to be used in this design had to be of small diameter, so they could fit side-by-side in the fuselage, thus giving it a flat cross-section, which would give good stability when the aircraft landed on the flexible deck. After various rocket and single jet engine installations were considered the decision was made to use the new Rolls-Royce axial-flow turbojet AJ.65 (AJ equating to 'Axial Jet', 65 denoted the projected thrust of 6,500lb), which was later named the Avon. Without undercarriage the wings could be manufactured to a finer profile, resulting in a 7% thickness/chord ratio for the Type 505, to the benefit of the projected performance and rate of climb. The thin wing had a thickness of 37.5% of the chord and was symmetrical with the aerofoil section constant across the entire 41ft span to avoid tip stalling. Fears about stalling also led to the radius profile of the leading edge of the wing being constructed as large as possible, to delay the breakaway of the airflow. The tail utilised a butterfly configuration to give better rigidity and strength in relation to its thin chord and thickness. It also ensured that the control surfaces were clear of the jet efflux, as it was feared that a conventional cruciform layout would be affected by exhaust gases. The use of the AJ.65 engines meant that the intakes could be positioned just aft and on either side of the cockpit, with the jet exhausts behind the wing trailing edge on either side of the fuselage. This afforded the engines the luxury of short exhaust pipes, which would reduce power loss, and also meant that the entire rear fuselage section was available for fuel tanks. Fore and aft control was achieved by moving the entire tail; elevators were installed to give additional pitch control. Differential movement of the elevators allowed the aircraft to turn and removed the need for a conventional rudder. The wings featured wide ailerons for lateral control with lift spoilers installed to assist during the approach stage of landing on a carrier. To aid recovery at high speeds dive brakes were installed under the wings at about one-third chord, their operation also had the added benefit of returning down-wash to the tail. Although it was not intended to have an undercarriage, the first machine was equipped with a fixed tricycle undercarriage to allow conventional landings during the initial performance trials. The cockpit was positioned well forward, as in the Attacker, giving the pilot excellent forward and downward vision. A cockpit pressure equivalent to 33,000ft was maintained at 40,000ft.

Tests with the flexible deck commenced at Farnborough in April 1945, when a pilotless glider was catapulted onto the experimental deck constructed above the runway. Two years passed before further research with the flexible deck concept was undertaken and De Havilland Vampire F.1 TG426, modified with an arrester hook and suitably strengthened fuselage, made a less than perfect landing with its undercarriage retracted on the flexible deck at Farnborough on the 29th December 1947. Sadly the approach by Lt Cdr Eric Brown OBE, DSC, AFC, was too slow and the arrester hook struck the ground pitching the aircraft onto its nose penetrating the flexible deck. The aircraft sustained considerable damage and was eventually written off, although thankfully Lt Cdr Brown was unhurt. Undaunted, on 17th March 1948 the first of 50 successful landings was made with Vampire F.1 TG286 and in November sea trails commenced on HMS *Warrior*. Two hundred landings were made with TG286 along with Sea Vampire F.21s VG701, VT795, VT802, VT803 and VT805. Even though these trials were considered by the RAE to have been concluded successfully, with only minor incidents reported, by this time it was considered by Admiralty that the flexible deck was incapable of being pursued as a worthwhile system offering no benefit over a conventional landing. The concept was dropped partly because there was insufficient time to allow the conversion of the aircraft carriers to accept aircraft without an undercarriage. Utilising the development work already undertaken by Supermarine, the DTD asked them to modify the design to a conventional tricycle undercarriage configuration as it was felt that the design could be adapted to meet a new specification. Initially the new specification, N.9/47, was intended as an alternative to the Hawker N.7/46, which later emerged as the Sea Hawk. In Supermarine's hands the new project was designated Type 508, a larger aircraft in comparison to the 505. It should be noted that even with the change of heart concerning the flexible deck, and with the Type 508 being required to have a conventional undercarriage, there was still a proviso in the specification that the 508 be capable of being converted to an undercarriage-less type for use on flexible deck carriers should

the fuselage because of the need to revise the engine mountings. The specification also called for an armament consisting of four 30mm ADEN cannon, provision for which was made under the air intakes. These weapons in the original Type 505 requirement were identified as MK213/30, as they were an ex-Mauser type not fully developed by the Germans in WWII but developed further in the UK during the immediate post-war period. Initially some consideration was given to adopt an escape 'capsule' in the form of a jettisonable cockpit, however this concept would have required much research and development and so was not pursued. Many discussions took place during the next six months between Supermarine, Rolls-Royce, the RAE, the RN and Air Ministry. On 4th June 1947 Sammy Hughes, the Chief Aerodynamicist at Super-

Supermarine Type 508 VX133 prior to the application of aerodynamic strakes from July 1952. Brian Lowe

the RN adopt it after all! Versions for both the RN and RAF were included in the specification, although for the purposes of this study only the RN requirement will be considered. The wing thickness ratio was increased from 7% to 9% creating a better lift co-efficiency and thereby reducing the landing speed to the required 105 knots laid out in the specification. The wings featured dive brakes in the form of spoilers on the upper surface of each wing and dive recovery flaps of 3.1sq ft on the under surfaces. An increase in all-up weight resulted in the wingspan being increased by 5ft, the wing area by 45sq ft (265 to 310sq ft) and the tail area by 13sq ft. In an attempt to save weight elsewhere the spar was run under the fuselage to take the undercarriage, thus changing completely the profile of

marine, prepared a report laying out the full requirements of the Type 508. Based on these requirements the Air Ministry issued a draft specification N.9/47 during August 1947 and Supermarine was asked to submit their Type 508 in relation to it. Both Hawker and Westland also submitted basic proposals for the Specification, but neither pursued them, as the Specification was almost written around the Type 508 in any case. Supermarine slightly revised their design, giving the 508 a span of 41ft, a length of 50ft, a folded height of 15ft 5in and a folded width of 19ft 6in; the Chief of Naval Research having asked Supermarine to reduce the original width of the 508 to 20ft back in May 1947. In this form the aircraft was to be powered by two Rolls-Royce Avon Mk 3s, producing

6,500lb of thrust each and this would result in a projected performance of 569kts at sea level, 511kts at 40,000ft and a service ceiling of 50,000ft. With this information to hand Specification N.9/47 was finalised to Naval Staff Requirement NR/A.17 on 22nd September 1947, although the weaponry was changed to consist of four 20mm Hispano Mk V or ADEN HV cannon. Ultimately a contract for three Type 508s, VX133, VX136 and VX138 was placed with Supermarine to Specification N.9/47 and contract number 6/Acft/1508/CB.7(b), on 3rd November 1947. Sadly, as was often the case at this time in British military aviation history, just a few months later, in early 1948, the armament requirement was revised to consist of four 30mm cannon with an added weight penalty of approximately 864lb. At the same time Rolls-Royce also informed Supermarine

facturer had concluded their checks of VX133, it was dismantled and moved by road to A&AEE Boscombe Down in Wiltshire. The first flight took place with Mike Lithgow at the controls from Boscombe Down on 31st August 1951. Although the gun ports for the 30mm cannon were fitted the guns themselves were not, and their weight was simulated with ballast during all flight trials. Operating from the nearby Supermarine test airfield at Chilbolton, Hampshire, the airframe managed to gather the minimum 10 hours of flying needed for it to take part in the 1951 SBAC event at Farnborough; although its display was kept to the minimum. The initial flight tests at A&AEE and Chilbolton proved that although the 508 had a high wing loading, the landing speeds though were within the Royal Navy's operating limits, due to the adoption of leading edge slats and large trailing edge flaps. Most of the test fly-

Opposite top: *VX133 with strakes clearly visible ahead of the tailplane.* via Tony Buttler

Opposite bottom: *VX133 in flight.* via Tony Buttler

Left: *On completion of its flying duties, VX133 was dispatched to RNAS Culdrose and received the instructional airframe number A2529. Shorn of its wings, the aircraft is seen here in the late 1960s at Culdrose.* Newark Air Museum

that the projected weight of each Avon was 400lb higher than originally envisaged! The direct result of this was that the design had now reached an all-up weight of 18,249lb with only 437 gallons of internal fuel. This was too heavy for the existing arrester gear and the required entry speed to the wire of 75kts in a 28kt wind was unobtainable and much of 1949 would be spent examining methods to overcome these problems.

Inspection of the Type 508 mock-up was undertaken in September 1948 and construction of the first prototype started in mid-1949. Some modifications were made before the prototype was completed, mostly as a result of wind tunnel tests. The spoilers on the wings were found to create disturbance at the tail and it was felt this may cause buffeting in flight, so they were modified. The first engine runs were undertaken at Hursley Park in June 1951. Once the manu-

ing centred around the evaluation of the leading-edge slats and trailing-edge flaps which led to the adoption of an interconnected system which, when full trailing-edge flaps were applied, 10° of leading-edge slats was also applied. Although take-off and rate of climb proved to be very good, the top speed was only 603mph (970km/h) at 30,000ft (9,144m), and there were various lateral and directional problems associated with the use of the butterfly tail. During a flight on the 5th December 1951, Mike Lithgow experienced violent accelerations of the aircraft, followed by a vertical upwards roll resulting in a peak stress of 11g, which caused him to pass out. On regaining consciousness he resumed control and landed. Subsequent inspection of the airframe revealed damage that included the loss of both wing tip pitots. A meeting between the manufacturer and the Air Ministry was convened on the 12th March 1952, to discuss the incident. Initial suspicions were focused on the servodyne control system, although tests proved this was not the case and it was discovered that 10 pints of oil had leaked from the hydraulic system by the time the aircraft landed. Checks revealed that this loss of fluid only slowed the operation of the undercarriage, but a stirrup fitting supporting the port wheel fairing was found to have failed leading to the port undercarriage door opening inadvertently. Modifications to the system were undertaken, with the alloy stirrup being recast in steel, the linkage operation of the leg and doors were also modified and a new undercarriage lock was installed. The aircraft left Chilbolton on the 29th April 1952 and flew to RAE Thurleigh in Bedfordshire to continue tests, and returned to Chilbolton on the 2nd May. It returned to Thurleigh on the 24th May for arresting trials, then flew back to Chilbolton on the 27th. The aircraft was then checked and flown to RNAS Ford, Sussex, before going on to HMS *Eagle* to undertake deck-landing trials. Seven landings were undertaken, all bar one (the second) was a success and this one was only considered a failure as the special cameras fitted under the airframe to film the operation of the undercarriage and arrester hook were turned off in error! Once the deck trials were concluded, VX133 returned to Chilbolton and had the test equipment removed so that it could continue the various manufacturer's trials.

During a display at the Lee-on-Solent, Hampshire, 'at home' day on 12th July 1952 the aircraft suffered severe vibrations that were soon identified as aileron oscillations. One of the main problems highlighted by the trials had been a tendency for the aircraft to 'snake' (directional oscillation) at medium and high speeds. To overcome this large strakes were added to the top of the rear fuselage immediately before the leading edges of the tailplanes so modifying the flow of air over this area. VX133 went back to Bedfordshire for measurement of landing loads during arresting trials on 15th April 1953, before returning to Chilbolton and was not finally accepted by the RAE until the 13th July and was eventually transferred to RAE Thurleigh on the 22nd August 1955. One of the last series of trials undertaken by VX533 was aboard HMS *Bulwark* from 31st October to 14th November that year. On 24th September the following year the airframe was moved by road to HM Dockyard Devonport for trials on HMS *Centaur* to test the ships hangar floor strength as it was intended to operate the type from this carrier in the future. VX133 returned to Bedfordshire on 28th November to continue arrester gear trials and was finally released by the RAE on 29th March 1963. In June, it was allocated to the Flight Deck Handling School at RNAS Culdrose, Cornwall, and allocated an Instructional Airframe number. The records show it on their charge by 31st October, but the airframe was not physically moved by road via Lee-on-Solent until the end of December that year.

Although three Type 508s were ordered, only VX133 was ever built and flown as such. The second prototype, VX136, was ordered as a Type 508, but was actually built as the sole Type 529. It joined VX133 at Boscombe Down for testing, undertaking its maiden flight from there on 29th August 1952. The 529 was basically similar to the 508 but was modified on the assembly line having benefited from data obtained during VX133's trials. It was also modified to accept armament. The airframe was 6in longer then its predecessor, mainly due to the extended tailcone that was installed for the proposed fitment of a radar warning system. Neither the armament nor radar was ever installed due to procurement problems and eventually the requirement was cancelled on 18th February 1953. Strakes, similar to those seen on VX133, extended forward 7ft from the butterfly tail and the arrester hook was simplified. Although the tailplane was similar to the 508 the whole tail cone was hinged at a point level with the leading edge of the tailplanes, to assist deck handling and storage. Both VX133 and VX136 went aboard HMS *Eagle* in October and November 1953 to undertake follow-on deck handling and landing trials. VX133 undertook normal landings to assess how easily service pilots would find the type in comparison with the Attacker, while VX136 undertook tail-down landings and catapult launch trials. Once these trials were concluded VX136 went to RAE Thurleigh and was allocated to the RN test Squadron there. Sadly the aircraft was damaged in an emergency landing with only the port leg down on 2nd December 1953 and the damage sustained was such that the aircraft was struck off charge eleven months later. After three years in storage the bulk of the airframe was moved to the Proof and Experimental Establishment (P&EE) at Shoeburyness, Essex, where it was finally destroyed in gunnery testing by 1961. It is interesting to note that the cause of the heavy landing on 2nd December was once again attributed to the same cause as Mike Lithgow's near accident with VX133 in December 1951, the undercarriage door coming open; Supermarine having assumed its modifications after that event had cured the problem! Although XV133 had the longest career, it also suffered an ignoble end. After its time at RNAS Culdrose, where it was used to train crews in moving aircraft on carrier decks, it was moved to Predannack were it was used for fire fighting training. Sadly, by the time its importance was realised in the early 1970s, the aircraft had been burnt beyond repair.

Above: *VX136 aboard HMS* Eagle *in October/November 1953.* via Tony Buttler

Below: *VX136 clearly displaying its tail section and strakes.* via Tony Buttler

Chapter 2: **TOWARDS THE SCIMITAR – TYPE 525 AND 544**

Type 525

As with the second Type 508, the third was modified sufficiently to be given a new type number, 525, and allocated the serial number VX138. The use of swept wings on aircraft intended to operate from carriers had, until the late 1940s, been considered unlikely due to the restrictions imposed particularly by the approach speed that a carrier-based swept-wing design would require. However, projected development in carrier arrester equipment and the adoption of various high-lift devices in swept-wing designs soon showed that such aircraft would become suitable for carrier operations. Since December 1948, Supermarine had been flying their swept-wing version of the Attacker, the Type 510, VV106 and from August 1951 they were also testing the Type 541, the first Swift prototype, again with a swept wing. It is not surprising therefore that Supermarine redesigned the Type 508 with a swept-wing. Discussions had taken place in April 1950 between Supermarine and the Air Ministry, in which the potential of the 508 to meet the N.9/47 specification was fully considered and after successful landings on HMS *Illustrious* by the Type 510 in November 1950, the Royal Navy was keen to have the swept wing 508. Supermarine had proposed the revised Type 508, featuring swept wings and tail in June 1949, but it was not until 1952 that real impetus was given to the project and it was allocated the previously unused type number 525. The new swept wings necessitated the movement of the undercarriage legs outboard and the extension of the oleo legs by 15in, without which, as the wing had no dihedral, the tips would have been too close to the ground. This also meant that the wing fold point moved outboard, although it remained within acceptable limits and would still fit current carrier deck lifts. The butterfly tail initially fitted was swept and this meant that the overall length increased from 50ft to 52ft 10in. Operational requirements for a high-speed jet on a carrier meant that high-lift devices had to be installed. On the 525 these were double-slotted flaps with extensions under the wings at the trailing edge and tapered slats along the leading edge. Lift spoilers were retained and Attacker-type dive brakes installed, plus dive recovery flaps at 0.3 chord width. The butterfly tail was soon discarded however due to structural problems associated with this unconventional empennage and replaced with a conventional cruciform unit that had an all-flying tailplane capable of moving through a 15° arc. The fin and tail junction was smoothed with a long fairing projecting backwards and this was used to house the three small-diameter braking parachutes. Apart from increased fuel capac-

Period advertisement for the Supermarine 525. via Author

ity, very little modification was needed to the original 508 fuselage or the Rolls-Royce Avon installation. Work to convert the partially built 508 to 525 standard had began in 1952 and most work was completed by the end of 1953. Initially it had been planned to move the incomplete airframe to A&AEE to appease the politicians, but Denis Webb, Assistant Experimental Department Manager argued that the potential costs of moving the airframe back should something go wrong at Boscombe Down, were far too great, and so it remained at Hursley Park until completed. This proved very fortunate, as during initial engine runs full power could not be achieved and Freddie Ballington from Rolls-Royce soon identified the problem as being caused by disturbance of the air in the intakes, thus preventing a smooth flow to the engines. The modifications took two weeks, but eventually the airframe was complete and after successful engines runs and very detailed checks of the route, the airframe, with undercarriage raised and outer wing panels removed, was taken by low-loader to A&AEE Boscombe Down to be made ready for its first flight. The journey took ten hours and after unloading at A&AEE on 25th April 1954 it was placed in a hangar. On the 26th the hydraulics and engines were tested, the compass was swung and it was pronounced fit to fly. Taxiing trials were undertaken by Mike Lithgow that afternoon and on the following day, 27th April, with Mike at the controls it made its maiden flight of 20 minutes in the company of Swift WK215 piloted by Dave Morgan. On the 29th, two further flights of 40 and 25 minutes respectively were undertaken by Lithgow, followed by a handling check flight on 6th May before the aircraft moved to Chilbolton that same day. VX138 was fitted with uprated Avon engines each of which produced 7,500lb of thrust, significantly more than those fitted to the 529. Although the extra power allowed the 525 to exceed the speed of sound in a shallow dive, having achieved Mach 1.08 on 1st November 1954, it remained subsonic in all other flight regimes and in some respects, in the climb for instance, was inferior to its straight wing predecessors. VX138 also proved to be unstable in certain attitudes, but these problems were overcome following modifications. The fin area was increased, and its leading edge redesigned and the control circuit modified. The aircraft was fitted with the proposed four ADEN cannon armament and tail radar system and, although not a great success, was an important evolutionary step towards the Type 544, which would later become the Scimitar. Significant development work was conducted with VX138 particularly when, following modification at Hursley Park, in June 1955,

the aircraft emerged with a flap blowing system. Designed to investigate boundary layer control, a system known by Supermarine as 'Super Circulation', directed a thin jet of high pressure air bled from the engine compressors and projected onto the aircraft flaps from a slot located along the trailing edge of the wing. This air, ducted from such powerful engines did not reduce performance, but bestowed the benefit of giving the aircraft a lower landing speed and also improved controllability whilst landing. The super circulation system reduced the approach speed by approximately 12mph as well as the necessary angle of attack on approach, thereby giving the pilot a better view of the flight deck. On 4th July 1955 VX138 moved to Boscombe Down, but sadly the following day it was lost in a fatal crash. The 525 was awaiting a carrier for landing trials, so Lt Cdr Tony Rickell, who was to be involved in the trials, was given the opportunity to familiarise himself with the aircraft. He undertook various low speed flights to investigate the handling of the 525 in the landing configuration and during his second simulated approach the aircraft stalled and spun into the ground. The pilot deliberately delayed his ejection in the hope of affecting a recovery until a point when the ejection system would not be 100% effective and he subsequently died of his injuries. The loss of the pilot and aircraft, just 15 months and 61 flying hours after its first flight, was a severe blow, especially as the type had failed to undertake any trials on a carrier. Although some

Above: Supermarine Type 525 VX138 (confirmed by the starboard engine blank), photographed at Boscombe Down in 1954. Author's collection

Below: VX138 presumably at the same location and date in unpainted condition. Brian Lowe

TOWARDS THE SCIMITAR – TYPE 525 AND 544   15

suspicion was aimed at the 'super circulation' flap-blowing system, this proved not to have been a contributing factor in the crash, however the loss of 525 had a very damaging effect on the whole project and in many ways can be seen to have delayed the development of the following N.113 project by a couple of years.

Type 544

Previous discussions concerning the Type 525 and the fact that it was felt it would not fully meet the requirements of Specification N.9/47 led to the issuing of a revision to specification N.113P (originally issued in July 1951) in May 1953 against contract 7/Aircraft/7784. This revised specification called for a single-seat fighter for interception, combat air patrols and long range daylight strike support from a carrier and able to operate by both day and night from shore bases.

Supermarine's revised Type 525 resulted in the Type 544, the first of which was built as N.113D (Development), serial number WT854. It was transported by road to Boscombe Down on 14th January 1956 and flown from there for the first time by Mike Lithgow just six days later in the company of Swift FR.5 WK277 flown by Dave Morgan. The aircraft undertook another series of test flights the next day before transferring a week later to the manufacturers airfield at Chilbolton. Supermarine were keen to regain lost time as a result of the premature demise of the Type 525, so WT854 was never fully representative of later 544s, as it was fitted with double slotted flaps instead of trailing edge flaps and super circulation. Also, it was without the revised profile vertical fin and extended rudder as fitted to the Type 525. WT854 also had its gun ports sealed, no doors fitted to the arrester hook bay and the tail bumper was locked in the down position. Initially the type was fitted with a large boom on the nose to contain the pitot and yaw vanes, but by the time it undertook carrier trials this had been removed. On 22nd March 1956 WT854 flew back to Boscombe Down to begin Aerodrome Dummy Deck Landings (ADDL), even though Mike Lithgow had serious misgivings about the stability and performance of the 544. By 5th April 38 landings had been undertaken and landing weights of 27,800lb to 28,200lb achieved. On 3rd April a team from Vickers and the Admiralty boarded HMS *Ark Royal*, while Mike Lithgow remained at Boscombe Down to fly WT854 to the vessel. Sadly, bad weather delayed the carrier for 24 hours and so it was not until the 5th that the 544 finally landed on *Ark Royal*. Lithgow experienced problems whilst landing in that he could not adequately see the landing mirrors and thus the hook struck the stern some four feet below deck level; thankfully without damaging the aircraft or the ship! Later flights showed the mirror system to be incorrectly set for this type of aircraft, resulting in the hook hitting the stern each time, but it could not be corrected as the mirror was already at its maximum height. WT854 undertook 29 deck landings on HMS *Ark Royal* during this first series of trials, seven with Mike Lithgow at the controls, nine each by Lt Cdr Colin Little and Lt Cdr Derek Whitehead and four by Cdr Stan Orr: the latter three pilots were from the A&AEE. All take-offs were accomplished without the benefit of the catapult system as the type had not been cleared for catapult launches by the RAE. During one flight on the 9th April, Lt Cdr Colin Little managed to complete the entire take-off run with the parking brakes still applied! The aircraft staggered over the bow and dropped towards the sea, but due to a combination of the pilot's efforts and ground effect, managed to struggle into the air, turn back and land on deck. This was not the first time this would happen, and it was discovered that the 'T' handle that operated the parking brakes was situated in such a position that once the pilot was fully strapped in he could not easily reach it. As a result the handle was subsequently moved from the bottom to the top edge of the instrument panel.

Two further Type 544s followed later in 1956, with WT859 flying for the first time on the 26th June and WW134 on the 10th October. In its intended role the type was to have been a single-seat fighter capable of long range strike support, but the changing military operational requirements of the era and the relatively poor performance at altitude meant that by the time it was being tested it was envisaged as a low-level strike aircraft capable of undertaking low altitude bombing sorties (LABS) and of carrying/delivering a nuclear weapon. The type had to display good control at low level, whilst remaining stable in the gusty air at that altitude. Control systems at this time, such as the Fairey power-controls were found to be over-sensitive at low level and so they had to be modified to provide better 'feedback'. The type also suffered from pitch-up which was worse than the 525 at high altitude and Mach numbers. This phenomenon was caused by the separation of airflow over the wing, which in turn led to high-speed tip stall. The situation was made worse by the all-flying tail-plane, which, with no independent elevators suffered from increased downwash because the airflow could not be deflected. The introduction of the saw-tooth wing leading edge, boundary-layer fences and the Kuchemann-shaped wing tips all contributed towards solving the problem, but with the 544 probably the most important change was from a 10° dihedral tailplane to 10° of anhedral. The stresses exerted on an airframe during a roll or pull-out were a major worry to Supermarine but they included many strengthening elements within the 544 which helped to ensure that the overall airframe was strong. These included high-tensile steel spars and rigid elements within high stress areas. They also opted to use Titanium in those areas that did not require strength but which did need to have high levels of heat resistance. All of this would add weight, so Supermarine adopted

Opposite top:
An undated view of VX138.
via Tony Buttler

Opposite bottom:
Mike Lithgow is seen climbing aboard VX138 at Farnborough for the 1954 SBAC event , the only time that this aircraft appeared there. Beyond is a Supermarine Swift and was probably the aircraft used to shepherd VX138 to and from the event.
Author's collection

Below: *Starboard view of Supermarine Type 544 WT854 in January 1956 as originally fitted with an extended nose boom.*

Port view of WT854 also in January 1956. The ejection seat warning triangle is situated on the aircraft's nose just below the cockpit sill; not to be confused with the triangle situated just behind the engine intake. The purpose or cause of the vertical ribbon like stripes on the aft fuselage is uncertain. Both Brian Lowe

chemical etching to remove surplus material, which was not only far more accurate, but was also far cheaper than conventional machining. The type did suffer from one major problem though – resonance fatigue in the rear fuselage. This was caused by the acoustic waves created by engine noise; Supermarine only overcame the problem by using thicker outer skins, and steel ribs to replace aluminium ribs and resin bonded foam-backed filling.

On 20th August 1956, while Mike Lithgow was flying WT854 back to Wisley he discovered that the nose leg would not fully extend. Despite use of the emergency systems the leg refused to fully extend and lock, so he had to land with the leg in this position. The subsequent emergency landing damaged the airframe, but not as badly as feared, and the fault was later traced to insufficient travel of the nose-wheel

sequence operating valve. Once the airframe had been repaired and fully modified with the anhedral tail it took part in the SBAC event at Farnborough, although it became unserviceable on the second day and the rest of the flying at the show was undertaken by Dave Morgan in WT859. Service handling and assessment trials were conducted with WT854 at Boscombe Down between 17th and 27th October 1956. WT859 was engaged in flight flutter trials from August to October 1956 and on 8th October was flown to Wisley for fitment of the Rolls-Royce Avon 202 engines and connection of the super circulation system, before returning to A&AEE for tests of said system. At the same time the third prototype, WW134, had joined the test programme. Being more representative of later production aircraft it had the anhedral tailplane, the wing fences and super

circulation system as well as a strengthened under-carriage and an aural indicator for approach speed. This was the first time the super circulation system could be tested on a carrier, as the Type 525 had been lost before it undertook trials and the previous two Type 544s were not fitted with a working system. Between November and December WT854 undertook the same series of ADDLs trials at A&AEE and Bedford, before moving to Plymouth for onward movement to HMS *Ark Royal* on 3rd January 1957. Bad weather restricted catapult launches to just five, all on 6th January, undertaken by Cdr Pat Chilton and Lt Cdr Derek Whitehead of 'C' Squadron, A&AEE and Mike Lithgow. Vickers were quite happy with the results of the trials, although the RN were less so as so few launches and landings had been achieved. During March and April tests were undertaken to check the temperature of the jet efflux pen-nib fairings which, it was discovered, rose to unaceptably high levels above Mach 1. Modifications were going to be inevitable. During May WT859 and WW134 were used by Mike Lithgow at Wisley for various handling trials with

WT859 used for handling with asymmetric power applied and lateral and directional tests, while WW134 was used to investigate behaviour at the stall. The report presented on 14th June highlighted that the stalling characteristics were acceptable but the view over the nose was poor during the approach due to the high angle of attack adopted. WW134 was tested in July (along with fourth production airframe XD215) with a cut-down nose ultimately incorporated in later aircraft from the first production batch. The aircraft was officially unveiled to Ministry and Royal Naval officials in November 1957 by which time they had undertaken 148 deck landings and catapult launches. It was found that the best approach speed was approximately 140mph at a weight of 28,000lb, the maximum permissible catapult launch weight was 34,000lb, where launch was achieved at approximately 134mph. In March 1958 WW134 was used to test the probe sensing unit of the Audio Incidence Indicator system and during October 1959 was used in connection with rough runway trials in relation to the TSR.2 programme.

At a later stage the nose boom was removed and WT854 undertook aircraft carrier trials aboard HMS Ark Royal as seen here in April 1954.
via Tony Buttler

By May 1958 WT854 was considered to be at the end of its flying life, so was put in storage at Wisley. Initially the Empire Test Pilot's School, RAE Farnborough, was interested in it, but this came to naught. Instead, the aircraft went to RAE Thurleigh and was used for non-flying arrester and bridle catching gear trials from 1958 until the beginning of 1960. The airframe was then scheduled to be sent to the RN Air Engineering School, at RNAS Arbroath, Angus, but this move was cancelled. In 1964 WT854 was moved by road to the School of Aircraft Handling, RNAS Culdrose, Cornwall, for the training of aircraft handlers. It remained there until 1967, when it moved to P&EE Shoeburyness and was expended there in various gunnery trials. WT859 also served with RAE Thurleigh, followed by the School of Aircraft Handling and finally the P&EE, but unlike WT854 it was not destroyed in ballistic trials at the latter location, and by 1991 when the various airframes at P&EE were disposed of, it was purchased by the Brooklands Museum, who removed the cockpit section and preserved it. The rough runway trials were the last active trials that WW134 was involved with, and in March 1962 it was flown to South Marston for future use in an Anglo-French

Underwater Sink-Rate Trial. Once flown to Toulon the engines were removed and the airframe was conveyed to HMS Centaur. Off the south of France the airframe was raised and lowered into the water for various trials to be undertaken, many involving underwater ejections of various Martin-Baker seats. By October 1962 the trials were at an end, having been immersed many times in salt water the airframe was unlikely to be of any further use, so the crew assembled on the flight deck and WW134 was catapulted off the ship and into a watery grave.

Opposite top: *The second Type 544 to fly was WT859 which first flew in June 1956.* Author's collection

Opposite bottom: *The third Type 544 to fly was WW134 in October 1956.* Author's collection

Above: *WW134.* via Tony Buttler

Chapter 3: **THE SCIMITAR IS BORN**

The name Scimitar was officially applied to the Type 544 in March 1957 and although an order for 100 was originally agreed, eventually only 76 were built, XD212-XD250, XD264-XD282 and XD316-XD333, with XD334-XD357 being cancelled. The first production airframe, XD212, made its maiden flight on 11th January 1957, at a time when all test flying of the Scimitar was moved from Chilbolton to Vickers' test airfield at Wisley. XD212, 213, 214 and 218 were all retained for varying periods, by the manufacturer for trials, while XD216, 217, 219, 226 and 228 all went to A&AEE Boscombe Down for armament trials. XD212 was used during a number of flights between 9th May and 13th June 1957 to determine if engine surge could be induced by firing the cannon. To reduce the time spent in undertaking these trials XD212 was fitted with a switch to allow either the port or starboard guns to be fired independently. Tropical trials at El Adem were undertaken with XD214, whilst XD229 spent its entire career with RAE Farnborough conducting various weapons trials over the ranges at West Freugh, Wigtown. XD215 undertook take-off performance and deck landing trials on HMS *Ark Royal* in the company of WW134 during the 18th to 25th July 1957. Both aircraft had been modified to improve the view over the nose during landing and in all 148 landings and catapult take-offs were achieved. Once completed, the pilots undertook two days of touch and go landings to see how the type

behaved both with and without super circulation in operation. Once the trials were concluded WW134 went back to A&AEE and XD215 to South Marston. Whilst XD217 was being flown by US Marine Corps pilot Captain Debencourt on the 18th September 1957 a loud thump was heard and a tendency to sideslip was noted. Observation from another aircraft noted that the fin was bent at about two-thirds height, but the pilot was able to make a successful emergency landing. Subsequent investigation never really determined the cause, as the fin was never identified as being weak, but a modification was introduced to provide additional strength across the entire span of the unit.

On the 14th October 1957, XD212, whilst being flown by Lt Cdr Abraham aborted a take-off from Wisley at the point of rotation and although the engines were cut and the brakes applied, the aircraft careered off the end of the runway, across a road before striking a lighting pole in an adjacent field. Investigation of this event determined that the unusual feel from the flight controls that had made the pilot abort the take-off was probably caused by contamination of the hydraulic system. Just a week later during a test on 21st October the control column of XD212 seemed to lock and the pilot needed both hands to move it. In flight the column seemed to easily 'stick' in one position, with moderate force needed to free it. The primary cause was again found to be contamination of

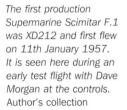

The first production Supermarine Scimitar F.1 was XD212 and first flew on 11th January 1957. It is seen here during an early test flight with Dave Morgan at the controls.
Author's collection

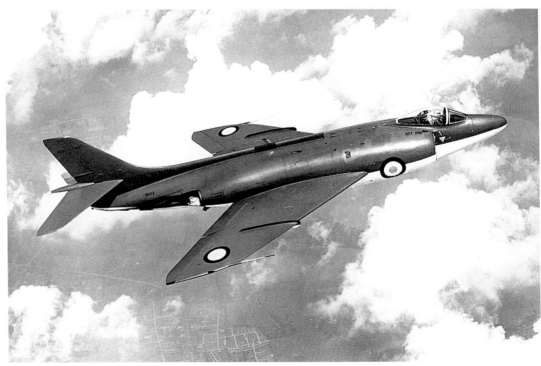

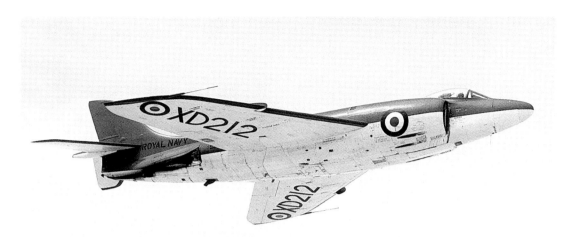

XD212, possibly on the same occasion as the preceding image. via Tony Buttler

F.1 XD226, possibly seen at Boscombe Down in 1958 where it was used in air speed sensing trials. The aircraft is devoid of any unit letters on the fin or three digit code on the fuselage, however, the solitary character '5' or 'S' is partially visible on the nose! Author's collection

the hydraulic system, so reconditioning of the hydraulic cylinders and valves along with flushing of the system was undertaken on the entire fleet and this was completed by the end of the month. Next the Scimitar was fully tested for performance, utilising WT859 and XD216. An absolute ceiling of 48,000ft was established with a rate of climb of 20,700ft/min at 5,000ft, 6,000 ft/min above 36,000ft and 1,000 ft/min at 46,000ft. The time taken to reach 45,000ft was 6 minutes 37 seconds. XD214 was used towards the end of 1957 to determine the effects of using 30° of flaps to augment the airbrakes during the descent. It was found that the flaps could not be used above 351mph, but their use in conjunction with the airbrakes below this speed reduced the decent from 20,000ft to 2,000ft by 1 minute 15 seconds as opposed to just using the airbrakes alone.

Time was also spent investigating problems created by a de-stabilising effect experienced when stores were carried on the outer pair of underwing pylons. The only way to correct the problem was to completely redesign all four pylons which resulted in new forward swept units being produced; these were first installed

on XD215. Drop tank jettison separation trials with the new pylons were undertaken with XD218 in January 1958 and found to be satisfactory. In May 1958 XD222 went to Wisley to take part in winterisation tests in the stratosphere chamber. Lt Read, a Royal Navy Project Officer with the cold weather trials group in Canada, headed the team. Because of the limited size of the chamber XD222 had the wings and nose folded and sections of the tailplane and vertical fin removed. The airframe remained in the chamber at -35° for sixteen days and a number of faults were noted. With the tests complete it was obvious that there were various system and servicing defects, which, uncorrected would cause damage to Scimitars operating in a low temperature environment.

During June 1958 XD218 commenced various Low Altitude Bombing System (LABS) related trials, and was in fact the only Type 544 to undertake such trials. Initially the trials centred around the familiarisation of the LABS technique, no actual LABS drops were made, the only drops were in level flight. These runs were conducted over the Orfordness ranges, but soon terminated due to complaints about noise and proximity to a bird sanctuary. As a consequence, further trials of the system were conducted at West Freugh from June 1959, where the LABS technique was tested taking advantage of its instrumented ranges. A total of 17 drops had been made by 10th July at angles of 45°, 60° and 100°.

In addition to weapons and other trials, the Scimitar needed to be subjected to an extensive series of demanding trials on board aircraft carriers. Therefore, trials aboard the newly-rebuilt and recommissioned HMS *Victorious* occurred between 29th August and 4th September 1958. Three Scimitars were involved, XD220, from No.700 Squadron which trialled an Audio Incidence Indicator (AII), XD221 and XD226 from the A&AEE, the latter fitted with and used for Air Speed Sensing Unit (ASSU) trials. These three aircraft completed dozens of launches with subsequent landings up to a maximum weight of 33,990lb, (the normal landing weight was 31,000lbs) several of which were undertaken using the AII and ASSU systems. One of the aircraft suffered damage to its arrester hook assembly, its 'A' frame being severely bent.

improvements. The first aircraft to fly incorporating these improved systems was XD276. A variety of systems problems were encountered with XD276 as it undertook flight testing, most of them in regard to systems not related to the new installations. Nine test flights were conducted before an acceptable level of reliability was achieved.

The first Type 560 Scimitar incorporating these modifications to undertake tropical trials was XD275. These trials were to be conducted at RAF Idris, Libya. Prior to departing from the UK XD275 suffered a serious hydraulic system fault on approach to landing at South Marston. Visual checks soon showed that the trailing edge flaps were in the fully up position and with no fuel for an overshoot the pilot opted to land without flaps. This he achieved and examination of the aircraft revealed that a hydraulic pipe had come off the flap jack, allowing the flaps to be blown up by the airflow. Once repaired the aircraft was sent to RAF Idris, arriving there in late summer 1959. In all some 37 sorties giving a total flying time of 24 hours were undertaken, with a maximum ground temperature of

F.1 XD222 609/LM of No.736 Squadron, RNAS Lossiemouth. This aircraft was used initially for cold weather trials at Wisley. K Darling via author

Various causes were considered but having examined marks on the flight deck caused by the hook at the point of touch down it was revealed that the hook had struck the side edge of the aft lift which projected approximately 1½in above the flight deck; a temporary fairing for the lift edge was considered sufficient to overcome this problem. Amongst the landings conducted, ten were undertaken under emergency wet weather conditions and each time the aircraft was inspected for signs of damage, although none was found.

Type 560

From XD275 onwards the Scimitar was modified to such an extent that it received a new type number, 560. Modifications included the adoption of Blue Silk, an improved version of the Green Salad airspeed and height indicator fitted to the first 50 production Scimitars, plus the installation of UHF radio and TACtical Air Navigation homing beacon (TACAN) amongst other

48°C being recorded! Phase 1 of the trials were successfully concluded on 4th August, with Phase 2 (photographic trials) being undertaken on 23rd August and 1st and 2nd September.

Many of the earlier production airframes were, by late 1959, returning to South Marston to be modernised. Sadly the modifications undertaken were not to the Type 560 standard and even though the RN were modifying service machines at this time with UHF to replace the VHF system, those 'modernised' by Vickers retained the older radio system!

The last Scimitar to roll off the production line at South Marston was XD333 at the end of 1960. This aircraft was over two months late for delivery due to the fact that many of the components needed for its completion had been inadvertently disposed off by an over-zealous storekeeper and said storekeeper was forced to go and recover them from the local scrap merchant to whom they were sold!

Above: *Culdrose 1957. An early production Scimitar offers external comparison with a Hawker Hunter.* via Tony Buttler

Below: *F.1 XD246 104/R of No.800 Squadron's aerobatic team, from HMS Ark Royal is seen at Lossiemouth in 1961. Visible behind the Scimitar's tail is the tail section of an Indian Navy Hawker Sea Hawk, bearing the single letter 'W'. A quantity of these aircraft remained in service with the Indian Navy until eventually replaced by the Sea Harrier.* Brian Lowe

Chapter 4: **SERVICE CAREER**

Training

Number 700X Squadron was the Scimitar Intensive Flying Training Unit which formed at RNAS Ford, Sussex on 27th August 1957 to train Scimitar pilots. Initially the unit was without Scimitars, so the pilots were seconded to Boscombe Down to undertake swept-wing flying training on Hawker Hunters. The first Scimitar delivered to the unit was XD221, but having suffered a bird strike during its initial delivery flight it was not re-delivered until 25th September 1957. In the event, XD221 became immediately unserviceable and remained so until 30th September. Despite this setback crew familiarisation flights had been concluded by the 17th October, following the delivery of XD220 on the 11th. From 24th October to 20th November the Scimitar fleet was grounded whilst they had their hydraulic systems checked and flushed (as previously recounted). The Flight was not only responsible for training crews it also had to amass as many flying hours in as short a period as possible, to iron out any problems with the Scimitar. To that end it was hoped to amass 300 hours on one airframe within six months. Sadly the unit lost its Commanding Officer, T G Innes AFC in a car accident near Arundel on 20th March 1958 and his place was temporarily filled by Senior Pilot Lt Cdr W A Tofts until Cdr J D Russell arrived to assume command. The unit remained the main Scimitar training unit until May 1958. On 21st May, four of the unit's Scimitars made noisy flypasts of Lee-on-Solent, Yeovilton, Bramcote, South Marston and Wisley prior to their final disbandment at Ford on 29th May. Some of the pilots and groundcrew remained with the unit, now designated No.700 Squadron, which later transferred to Yeovilton having concluded carrier trials with the Scimitar and HMS *Victorious*. Most squadron personnel however, along with their remaining aircraft, became part of No.803 Squadron when it formed at Lossiemouth on 3rd June 1958. Number 700 Squadron ceased using the Scimitar in February 1959.

Although No.700 Squadron had received Scimitars by the simple expedient of No.700X becoming No.700 Squadron in May 1958, the next training squadron to equip, partially at least, was No.764 Squadron. Its first Scimitar F.1 was received in February 1959. The intention originally was that this would become the principal unit conducting conversion and weapon training courses for those pilots due to be posted to Scimitar squadrons. This policy was changed however and No.736 Squadron adopted this role instead. Number 764 had relinquished its Scimitars by May 1959, and received the Hawker Hunter T.8 instead.

As the Naval Air Fighter and Strike School, No.736 Squadron received six F.1s in June 1959. This squadron remained in this role until disbanded on the 26th March 1965, although a small number of its personnel remained to become No.764B Squadron.

Formed on the same day that No.736 Squadron disbanded, and maintained as a Flight, No.764B was the only other training unit to use the Scimitar. Its tasks included army co-operation, to assist with aircraft carrier work-up periods and to train the pilots from Airwork Limited to fly the Scimitar. It was disbanded on the 23rd November 1965 having completed its allotted tasks. Numbers 736, 764 and 764B Squadrons were all based at Lossiemouth (excluding temporary deployments) whilst equipped with the Scimitar.

OPERATIONAL SQUADRONS

No.803 Squadron

The first operational squadron to equip with the Scimitar was No.803 Squadron at Lossiemouth on 3rd June 1958 under the command of Cdr J D Russell. A number of the pilots had previously served with No.700X Squadron and were familiar with the Scimitar. Aircraft from the squadron visited RNAS Ford in June, received a visit from the First Sea Lord on the 10th July, conducted flying displays at their home base, at Eglinton, Londonderry and the SBAC show at Farnborough. All aircraft had returned to Lossiemouth by 11th September and after a period of weapons training they left, in pairs, on 23rd to embark on HMS *Victorious*. Tragically, their commanding officer, although first to make a perfect landing on the carrier, was lost when the arrester wire parted and the aircraft went into the sea. The Search And Rescue (SAR) helicopter was there instantly, but the pilot could not be extracted. All the remaining aircraft were waived off and returned to Yeovilton. Following checks the Commander Air aboard HMS *Victorious* decided to let the rest of the squadron land on the carrier to which they returned. Lt Cdr G R Higgs later took over as the new CO. The ship moved into the Mediterranean and between the 6th and 8th October the squadron, in concert with Sea Venoms, undertook exercises off Gibraltar. The carrier arrived at Malta on the 13th and left the following day. After a visit to Toulon, the carrier was back at Malta on 7th November. After a period ashore due to catapult problems on *Victorious*, the squadron embarked once again on 10th December, only to be grounded for checks after Lt Maina, in XD237, lost half of his port jet pipe during the flight out to the ship. The carrier sailed for the UK on 2nd

Above: *The first squadron to receive the Scimitar was No.700X Squadron based at Ford (FD). This unit was allocated the codes 800 to 809 inclusive, although it is understood that only 800 to 806 was allocated to the Scimitars, the last three being assigned to De Havilland Sea Vampire T.22s which were also part of the Squadron's complement. 805/FD's serial number isn't revealed, although the types propensity to leak is, even at this early stage, 1957; revealed by the dustbins located beneath the rear fuselage. FAA Museum*

Below: *F.1 XD226 510/VL (Yeovilton), No.700 Squadron, seen at Yeovilton in 1958/59, to which location the Squadron had moved in September 1958. One of the dustbins below its fuselage is a little more mobile as it appears to have been secured to a handcart! The neighbouring aircraft to 510/VL is Sea Hawk FGA.4 WV904 516/VL, also of No.700 Squadron, whilst beyond that are several visiting Scimitars from No.803 Squadron. FAA Museum*

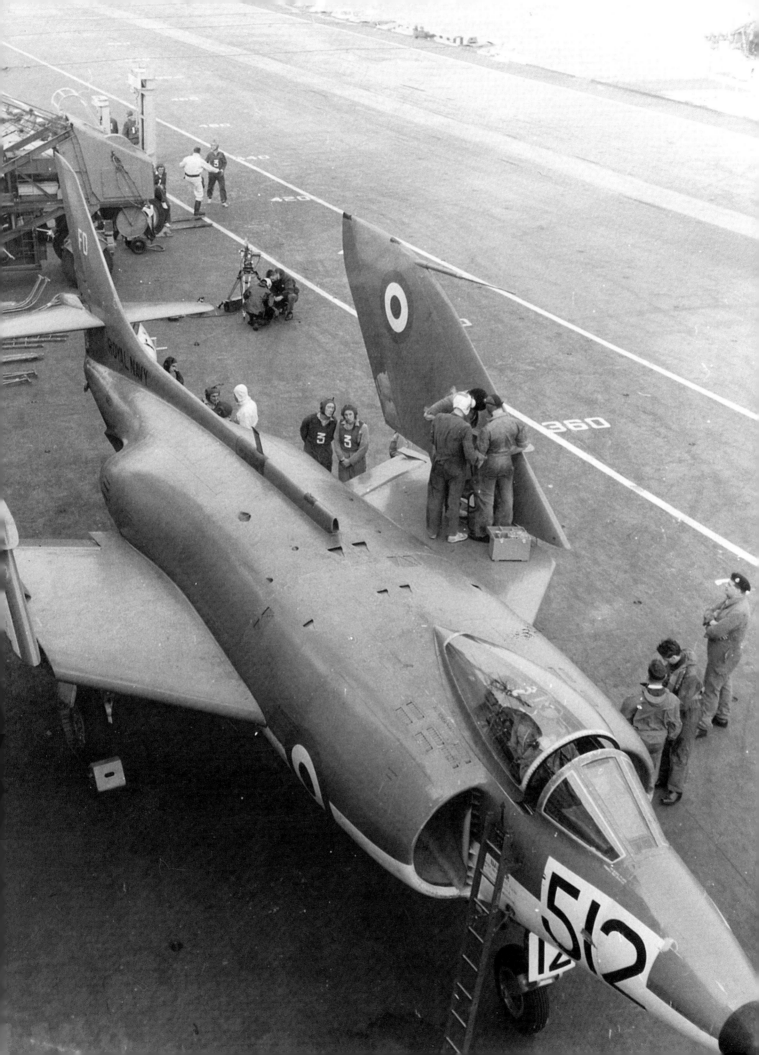

January 1959, calling at Gibraltar on the 9th and 10th, half the squadron disembarked to Lossiemouth on the 13th. They returned to the carrier on 21st February and set sail for Gibraltar, arriving there on the 25th, then moved off for exercises in the Western Mediterranean. It returned to Gibraltar on 6th March, then took part in exercise *Dawn Breeze 4* before returning to Portsmouth on the 24th, No.803 having returned to Lossiemouth the previous day. On 1st May ten aircraft from the squadron flew to Yeovilton and from there embarked on *Victorious* three days later. The carrier undertook a number of visits to bases in the UK and Europe, including a royal visit to *Victorious* by King Olaf of Norway on 18th June before returning to Portsmouth on the 22nd. For most of July the carrier visited various locations in the USA returning home on the 9th August. After re-embarking on 15th September the squadron spent the rest of that year visiting Norway, Gibraltar, Malta and Marseilles, as well as taking part in joint-exercises with RAF Canberras and the US Navy carrier, USS *Saratoga*. When they returned to Lossiemouth on 14th December, Lt Cdr A J Leahy MBE, DSC took over as Commanding Officer. Most of 1960 was spent shore-based at Lossiemouth, but the squadron did embark on *Victorious* for exercises in February before the ship went to Portsmouth for a refit on 25th February. The squadron suffered one fatal crash, one serious injury plus another crash whilst shore-based during the next three months. The Squadron did not embark *Victorious* again until 21st October for visits to Gibraltar, Malta and Naples and participation in exercises *Royal Flush* and *Pink Gin*. XD329 was lost on 9th December, but the pilot was recovered unharmed and the carrier returned to the UK with the squadron disembarking to Lossiemouth on 18th December. During the Christmas break Lt Cdr T C S Leece took over as Commanding Officer.

Returning to *Victorious* on the 20th January 1961, the carrier sailed for a ten-month deployment to the Far East on the 30th. It sailed via Gibraltar to Gambia and on to Cape Town, arriving there on 17th February. It then moved on to Aden, 11th to 18 March, Singapore, 4th to 17th April and on to Pulau Tioman off the east coast of Malaysia prior to taking part in exercise *Pony Express*. Sadly, XD273 was lost on 28th April and the pilot, Lt G C Edwards, later died of his injuries at Changi Hospital. On 8th May the Scimitars disembarked to RAAF Butterworth, Borneo, whilst the carrier docked at Singapore. The political situation then developing in the Persian Gulf was such that the carrier was required to attend the area as rapidly as possible, duly arriving off the Kuwaiti coast on 9th July. The Scimitars were sent ashore to operate from Almadi and Farwania airfields in Kuwait itself as neighbouring Iraq had made aggressive overtures; this was the closest the Scimitar ever came to being used in anger. The squadron did loose one aircraft, XD269, whilst patrolling over the Gulf, but its pilot Lt McIntyre

was picked up unhurt by the SAR helicopters. On 31st July *Victorious* was replaced by HMS *Centaur* and withdrew from the Gulf. The carrier then visited Mombasa and Aden before returning to Singapore where the squadron disembarked to RAF Tengah on 14th September. Number 803 Squadron had returned to the carrier by 5th October, and visited the Philippines for an exercise in company with the USS *Ticonderoga*. The carrier returned to Singapore in early November and on the way back to the UK undertook a mercy mission to deliver aid to Mombasa, before moving north to Aden and then via the Suez Canal back into the Mediterranean for an exercise off Malta. The squadron left the carrier whilst off Sardinia on 9th December and flew back to Lossiemouth via Yeovilton for the Christmas period.

The squadron's last tour aboard *Victorious* commenced when the squadron embarked on 5th February 1962. The carrier then visited Brest between 15th and 19th February, before moving to Gibraltar and then to Vigo, Spain between 17th and 22nd March. After an exercise in the area the carrier headed back to the UK and the squadron disembarked to Lossiemouth on 30th March. In April No.803 Squadron undertook carrier deck trials on HMS *Hermes* and embarked on 25th May before the ship sailed for the Mediterranean. It arrived at Malta on 4th June where seven Scimitars were disembarked to Hal Far, then undertook a short visit to Beirut between 5th and 9th July before returning to the island on the 20th. On 14th July XD213 suffered a bird strike whilst being flown by Lt N M Tristram. The bird penetrated and shattered the windscreen and stuck the pilot in the face and despite being almost blinded with slivers of perspex he managed to land safely aboard his ship. For this feat, Lt Tristram was awarded the Queens Commendation for Brave Conduct. On the 27th July *Hermes* arrived at Gibraltar and Lt Cdr N J P Mills took command of the squadron from 1st August. On the 9th No.803 re-embarked and set sail to take part in exercises with the aircraft carriers USS *Enterprise* and *Forrestal*. XD331 was lost on the 13th, although the pilot Lt Cdr B Wilson, was picked up unhurt by an escorting frigate. The carrier visited Lisbon between 16th and 18th and Palma between 23rd and 27th August before returning to Malta to take part in an exercise with the French Navy. On 2nd October the carrier sailed for the UK with the Scimitars leaving the carrier *en route* to return to Lossiemouth. Arriving in the UK on 5th November *Hermes* remained at berth until the 12th and No.803 re-embarked on the 13th for another tour of the Far East. After visiting Gibraltar and taking part in exercises, it moved through the Suez Canal and called at Aden between 8th and 9th December before finally arriving at Singapore on 21st December.

The carrier left Singapore on 6th January 1963 with just nine Scimitars aboard to conduct exercises and visits in the Far East before returning to

Opposite: *F.1 XD221 512/FD, No.700 Squadron, 1958, embarked for trials. This unit had been issued the codes 500 to 524 to cover its fleet of various aircraft types of which, 510 to 512, were allocated to its Scimitars. FAA Museum*

Opposite top: *F.1s XD224 615/LM (Lossiemouth) and XD230 617/LM, No.736 Squadron, in mid-1960. This unit utilised the codes 600-625 during the period 1956 to March 1965, within which, the Scimitars received the codes 608 to 618 from June 1959 when the first Scimitars were received, until March 1965 when it was disbanded. The Squadron's few remaining Sea Hawk FGA.6s were relinquished to 738 Squadron by June 1960. XD224 is seen with two underwing pylons fitted in comparison with the four on XD230.*
Author's collection

Opposite bottom: *F.1 611/LM, No.736 Squadron, seen at Lossiemouth. Neither the serial number or date is supplied, however, the fin of the neighbouring Scimitar displays the blue lightning flash on a white background which replaced the tail code LM from 1961. The last two digits of the aircraft's code number 611, is displayed on the nose-wheel door.*
FAA Museum

Portsmouth on the 29th July 1963. Following a period of exercises five aircraft were put ashore at Yeovilton one of which, XD213 crashed near Weymouth on 20th September. From 26th September No.803 was back aboard *Hermes* and deployed to the Mediterranean before returning to the UK and the squadron disembarking to Lossiemouth on 22nd October.

Number 803 Squadron spent most of 1964 shore based at either Lossiemouth or Yeovilton with only brief periods spent at sea. On 25th February 1964 No.803 acquired the Scimitars from No.800 Squadron which disbanded on that day, increasing No.803's complement of Scimitars to 16. It gained a new CO, Lt Cdr P G Newman on 4th May and took part in the FAA Jubilee Review at Yeovilton on 28th May. The squadron was also to take part in the SBAC show that year and during early December it undertook deck landing practice on HMS *Ark Royal*.

The squadron embarked on HMS *Ark Royal* on the 23rd January 1965 to begin a work-up period during February and March, before it disembarked and returned to Lossiemouth on 16th March, where it remained until the unit re-embarked just prior to *Ark Royal* sailing for the Far East on 17th June. The carrier arrived at Gibraltar on 22nd June, passed through the Suez Canal on the 28th and arrived at Aden on 2nd July, then onwards to Singapore via Penang, arriving on 19th July. XD328 engaged the barrier and was written off on 30th August, although the pilot Lt N Rankin, was unhurt. After exercising with USS warships *Ark Royal* returned to Singapore and the squadron disembarked to RAF Changi, before moving on to RAAF Butterworth on 10th November. During their time at Butterworth one aircraft was lost, but the pilot ejected safely and the squadron returned to Changi on 22nd November. The squadron went aboard again on the 7th December and spent Christmas in Fremantle, Australia, although the year's end was marred by the loss of XD318, although the pilot Lt Williams ejected safely.

HMS *Ark Royal* returned to Singapore in the New Year and the squadron disembarked to Changi. Between the 2nd January and 17th February the Squadron lost three Scimitars all of which were piloted by Sub Lt Z K Skrodski. The three aircraft involved were XD279, XD316 and XD250. XD279 was involved in a deck incident on 1st January 1966, when, having been released from the arrester wires the aircraft slid as the ship heeled and XD279 ran off the deck-edge, its nose-wheel going into the cat-walk. The damage sustained was significant and eventually resulted in the aircraft being written-off and reduced to spares recovery. XD316 was abandoned on 28th January when the nose pitched-up as the aircraft approached *Ark Royal* to land and the pilot was unable to recover and ejected. The third of the three incidents occurred on 17th February when XD250 suffered a hydraulic failure and fire 30 miles from the ship, again Skrodski was forced to eject. The carrier and squadron

visited Mombasa in February, with a spell of Beira Patrols on the way back to Singapore. The squadron lost XD325 when it engaged the barrier on 7th March and was damaged beyond repair. After disembarking to Changi, No.803 Squadron lost XD277 off the coast near Changi and XD323 due to damage caused after a nose-wheel collapse. XD277 was lost on 6th April, when the fire warning lights came on just after take-off. The pilot, Lt De Souza stayed with the aircraft long enough to direct it safely out to sea before ejecting. *Ark Royal* went out to relieve *Eagle* and undertake Beira Patrols and was itself relieved by *Victorious* on 25th May. On her way back to the UK *Ark Royal* made the last visit by a British carrier to Aden, then travelled via the Suez Canal on 4th June before No.803 Squadron left the carrier and returned to Lossiemouth on the 12th. The squadron's last tour on *Ark Royal* commenced on 2nd August for an exercise off Norway, followed by a visit to Oslo and finally back to Portsmouth to take part in the Navy Day event. The squadron was visited on the carrier by the Queen Mother on 20th September, following which the squadron disembarked and officially disbanded on 1st of October 1966. Number 803 Squadron was equipped with the Scimitar for a little over eight years, a longer period of use than any other squadron or unit.

No.807 Squadron

No.807 Squadron was the next operational unit to receive the Scimitar and re-formed at Lossiemouth on 1st October 1958 under the command of Lt Cdr K A Leppard. The squadron had received its first two Scimitars, XD243 and XD244, two days earlier and these were later joined by XD245 through to XD250 inclusive, XD245 having arrived on 4th October. The squadron took part in an exercise during the 16th to 18th October, even though by then there were still only four Scimitars on strength. The squadron suffered its first loss quite soon, with Lt C R Cresswell dying from injuries sustained after inadvertently being ejected from his aircraft after a mid-air explosion. The Scimitars were grounded as a result of this incident, and although this was lifted on 26th November another accident on HMS *Victorious* led to them being grounded again on 12th December. Once this order was lifted on 16th December training was resumed training and on 19th January 1959 the squadron completed 20 sorties in one day! For the remainder of 1959 the squadron remained principally at their home base although detachments were sent to West Freugh between 27th and 29th January and 7th to 9th July and Yeovilton, 9th to 12th June, as well as participating in flying displays at RNAS Culdrose on 25th June and the annual SBAC event at Farnborough 2nd to 15th September. On 22nd September command was handed over to Lt Cdr W A Tofts and the rest of the year was spent in training and exercises. Lt N Grier-Rees had to eject from XD281 when the controls locked during a flight over the Highlands on 19th

November; this was the first successful ejection from a Scimitar. 1960 began with training at Portsmouth, followed by a two aircraft detachment to HMS *Victorious* for deck landing trials from 20th to 23rd January. In early February two more crews, including the CO, went aboard HMS *Ark Royal* for deck wire-pulling trials and on 3rd March the entire squadron went aboard HMS *Ark Royal* for work-up in the Mediterranean. No.800 Squadron was also aboard at this time and marked the first occasion that two Scimitar squadrons were operational aboard the same carrier at the same time. The carrier arrived at Gibraltar on 7th March and then departed on the 9th for Malta, arriving in Grand Harbour on the 11th. During the rest of March and the beginning of April the carrier undertook trials off Marsaxlokk, Cyprus, with a visit to Palermo, Sicily on 25th March before returning to Malta, where a detachment to Hal Far commenced on 8th April through to the 18th. The squadron took part in a number of exercises, with a return to the island on 2nd May before heading back to Gibraltar for a visit from 5th to 20th May. After this it went to Toulon 28th May and left there on the 30th for another exercise before anchoring off Barcelona, Spain, from 3rd to 8th June. The Scimitars were joined by Aéronavale Aquilons (license-built Sea Venoms) on 11th June for deck landing practice. These aircraft left the next day, having lost one pilot in an accident. Between exercises on 15th to 17th June and 11th to 19th July, the carrier went back to Gibraltar for maintenance. Further exercises were conducted during the next two months, with a return to Malta on 29th July and a visit to Palma, Majorca, before the carrier headed home on 22nd August, arriving back at Rosyth on 5th September for further maintainance. Once completed *Ark Royal* headed north for Arctic trials and, incidently, became the first British carrier to sail close to the pack ice off Greenland. On 30th September all the fixed-wing aircraft left the carrier and flew back to their respective bases, but were back aboard by the 26th October and headed for the Mediterranean once more. Both No.800 and No.807 Squadron's Scimitars were once again embarked simultaneously. The carrier arrived at Gibraltar on the 30th, stayed for two days then set course for Malta, arriving there on 4th November. Scimitars were required ashore, and so *Ark Royal* made history by launching two No.807 Squadron Scimitars on 12th November, the first time a jet had taken off from a carrier whilst moored in the harbour. The squadron went back aboard on the 14th November and then took part in a number of exercises before the crews disembarked on Malta in mid-December to spend Christmas there.

1961 started with participation in an exercise before sailing for the coast of Spain. The carrier then moved north for further Arctic trials, following which the ship visited New York from 18th to 22nd February before heading back across the Atlantic and home. The squadron departed *Ark Royal* for the last time and

returned to Lossiemouth on 27th February in company with No.800's Scimitars. Three aircraft went aboard *Centaur* on 5th April with the remainder joining them on the 10th, as the carrier made its way to Gibraltar, arriving there on the 13th. *Centaur* moved to the Malta area from the 19th to work-up and entered Grand Harbour on the 29th. The second stage of work-up commenced on 8th May, followed by participation in an exercise the next day and more trials in the Malta and Marsaxlokk areas. After a brief stay at Messina during 19th to 22nd May, the carrier returned to Malta on the 25th for its third and final stage of work-up. After a joint exercise with the US Sixth Fleet the carrier headed for Spain, visiting Barcelona from 2nd to 7th June 1961. Next the carrier moved to the Toulon area for further exercises, before returning to Gibraltar on the 14th. The crisis in the Persian Gulf and the threat to Kuwait, resulted in *Centaur* being dispatched to the area, reaching Aden by 9th July. Sailing again on the 21st, *Centaur* eventually reached the Persian Gulf to relieve *Victorious* on the 31st. Here, No.807 Squadron Scimitars undertook patrols off the coast of Kuwait, although *Centaur* only remained in the area for a short while before returning to Aden in order to collect XD282, which had suffered brake failure at Khormaksar and then headed for the Mediterranean, via Suez on the 20th August before the Scimitars of No.807 Squadron flew off on the 27th to Hal Far. The squadron did not remain there long, as they all (except XD282, which was returned to the UK aboard *Centaur* for repair) headed back to Lossiemouth on the 31st. The squadron returned to *Centaur* on 20th October and after a period of weapons training at Aberporth, Cardigan Bay, the carrier sailed for the Far East. It arrived at Gibraltar on 31st October, then moved on to Toulon and arrived at Marsaxlokk on the 12th. The squadron went ashore to Hal Far on the 15th, and then rejoined the carrier on the 27th before sailing to Mombasa where it arrived on 1st December. The squadron remained there for Christmas while the carrier underwent maintenance. *Centaur* set out on the 27th and New Year was spent at Aden before arriving at Hong Kong on 17th January 1962.

The squadron participated in exercises during early January. Four Scimitars were flown to RAF Tengah on the 31st, they remained in the Far east as a source of spare aircraft each to the latest fully modified standard. The squadron in return received older, less modified examples for eventual return to the UK. On 1st February the remainder of the squadron disembarked to RAF Tengah, but left the base once again and joined the carrier as it headed for home on the 19th. Taking part in an exercise during early March the squadron lost XD319 off Aden on the 7th when the pilot Sub Lt A D Alsop attempted to go around having missed the wire, but sadly failed to gain any height and ditched ahead of the carrier. Thankfully the pilot escaped before the aircraft sank and was picked up

*F.1 XD276 100/R
HMS Ark Royal, No.800
Squadron. Reformed in
July 1959, this unit
received codes numbering
from 100 to 113 inclusive.*
Newark Air Museum

by the SAR helicopter. As part of the Far East Fleet *Centaur* arrived at Pulau Langkawi on 10th March, left two days later and arrived at Aden on the 23rd where No.807 Squadron disembarked for Khormaksar. They were all back aboard by the 30th as the carrier left Aden on 4th April 1962. It visited Istanbul between 7th and 11th April and Tripoli between 12th and 16th before returning to Grand Harbour, Malta on the 18th and the Scimitars then flew to Hal Far. Four aircraft flew from Hal Far directly back to Lossiemouth on the 26th while the rest of the squadron re-embarked onto *Centaur* on the 30th. The carrier departed on 3rd May and reached Gibraltar on the 9th, it left again on the 11th and arrived at Spithead on the 15th where No.807 Squadron disbanded.

No.800 Squadron

The third operational squadron to be equipped with the Scimitar was No.800 Squadron, which formed at Lossiemouth on 1st July 1959. Commanded by Lt Cdr D P Norman, it remained at Lossiemouth for the rest of 1959 and part of 1960 to undertake intensive training on the new aircraft. It embarked on *Ark Royal* on 3rd March 1960, and undertook a tour in the company of No.807 Squadron's Scimitars, as recounted elsewhere. During this period XD280 was seriously damaged after the pilot, Lt P E H Banfield, engaged the barrier due to undercarriage failure. The squadron left *Ark Royal* for Lossiemouth on 30th September 1960, rejoining the vessel on 26th October until returning to Lossiemouth on 27th February 1961, in company with No.807's Scimitars. It was then chosen to become the Royal Navy Display Team, called 'The Red Blades' and participated in various shows including the Paris Air Show in June and the SBAC show at Farnborough in September. Returning to Lossiemouth on 15th September the squadron's complement was raised from six to twelve aircraft and on 2nd October the CO changed, with Lt Cdr A Mancais taking over. The Scimitars were then subject to the modifications necessary to allow their Scimitars to operate Bullpup

and Sidewinder missiles. Once the crews had become proficient ten aircraft embarked on *Ark Royal* for work-up in the Mediterranean. The aircraft undertook intensive weapons training off the coast of Marsaxlokk before returning to Lossiemouth on 10th January 1962. Number 800 Squadron now possessed a significant strike capability.

During the next couple of months the squadron strength was increased to fourteen aircraft and re-embarked *Ark Royal* on 10th March. It arrived in the Malta area on the 15th where the squadron undertook training and participated in an exercise before the ship sailed for Aden. This marked the start of a Far East detachment, with Aden being reached on the 27th, whereupon the squadron spent the next four days taking part in day and night flying exercises. On 31st March the carrier travelled through the Straits of Malacca, with joint exercises in conjunction with the RAAF from Butterworth in the Penang area during the period 9th to 11th April, before the carrier arrived at Singapore on the 12th. *Ark Royal* set sail again on 24th April 1962 following a period of maintenance, and took part in exercises with the Royal Marine Commandos and the Australian, New Zealand, Pakistan and US navies. It arrived at Manila Bay on 2nd May, then on to Subic Bay on the 5th for an exercise with the US Seventh Fleet, then on to Hong Kong, arriving on the 17th. The carrier set course on 5th June for Japanese waters, arriving at Okinawa on the 9th, before sailing once more on the 16th to take part in exercises in the area. It was during these exercises that the first firing of Bullpup missiles by frontline RN aircraft was achieved by Lts Howard and Marshall. After the exercise the carrier returned to Singapore and five aircraft from No.800 Squadron went ashore to RAF Tengah. These machines returned to the carrier so it could take part in an exercise on 12th July, by the 26th six aircraft had returned to Tengah. It was during a landing here on 1st August that Lt Ellis the pilot of XD278 had to engage the barrier on the airfield due to partial brake failure and the aircraft was so badly damaged that it had to be left behind. The carrier sailed once again on 6th August, arriving at Fremantle, Western Australia, on the 20th. Six aircraft from the squadron were flown ashore to RAAF Pearce for ten days, before the carrier headed back to Singapore arriving on 13th September. It departed Singapore on the 20th and took part in Army and Royal Marine exercises on the Asahan Ranges, before making its way to Hong Kong and anchoring at Green Island on 5th October. It left the area on the 12th and headed back to Singapore, while en-route flying training continued and another exercise was undertaken over the Asahan Range. The carrier reached Singapore on the 19th, then left for home on the 24th, visiting Aden and Mombasa, reaching Gibraltar 10th December and finally Plymouth by the 14th where the squadron disembarked and flew back to Lossiemouth for Christmas.

With the squadron complement reduced to twelve aircraft, 'A' Flight embarked on Ark Royal on the 19th February 1963 for exercises in the Western Approaches, before returning to Devonport on the 28th, then setting course again on 7th March for an exercise from the 9th to 14th March before the Flight went home on the 16th. Command of the squadron was temporarily taken by Lt Cdr Mills until on the 5th March the post was filled by Lt Cdr P Newman. The whole squadron now with its full complement of fourteen aircraft left the UK on 4th May to rejoin Ark Royal, steaming off the Balearic Islands after a refit at Gibraltar. XD239 was lost in Aden Bay on 22nd May and its pilot, Sub Lt C D Legg, sustained back injuries in the ejection, while XD321 had brake failure after landing on Ark Royal and taxied into one of the anti-aircraft gun mountings on the 31st. During a stay at Mombasa, five aircraft from the squadron were detached to Embakasi from 7th to the 19th June. The squadron re-embarked and set course for Singapore and, during an exercise, suffered a fatality when Lt MacFie crashed behind the carrier on 31st July whilst attacking the 'splash target'. Back in the Singapore area, seven aircraft were detached to Tengah from 7th to 29th August, with XD221 Sub Lt McMeekan engaging the barrier there on the 24th and was left behind due to the damage sustained. The carrier again took part in exercises in the Singapore area before making a visit to Hong Kong from 6th to 12th September 1963. A further exercise took place from 16th to 21st September, before a short visit to Singapore, followed by RAAF Butterworth on 23rd and finally leaving the Far East region on the 26th. Returning to the Middle East the carrier visited Khor al Fakkan in the Gulf of Oman from 5th to 7th October, then took part in a tri-service exercise from the 7th to the 12th. The carrier returned to Mombasa and five aircraft again went ashore to Embakasi from 18th October until 1st November. In the company of USS Essex, HMS Ark Royal anchored off Karachi on 9th November and took part in an exercise there from the 14th to the 23rd (the exercises being cut short by the announcement of the assassination of President Kennedy on 22nd November). Ark Royal left the area on the 23rd and made its way to Aden, arriving on the 29th so the squadron could take part in the Khormaksar Air Day. After this the carrier moved off to Zanzibar, arriving on 4th December, where the crew acted as Guard of Honour for Prince Philip during the independence celebrations. The carrier then sailed to Mombasa, arriving on the 11th and departing on the 14th, this time for the independence celebrations of Kenya. The squadron finally left the carrier and flew home on the 31st December 1963.

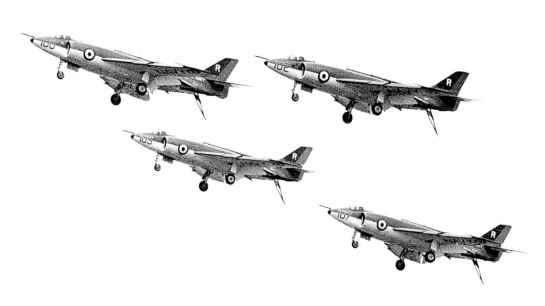

SBAC Air Show, Farnborough 1961. Four of the nine Scimitars which No.800 Squadron displayed at that event are seen in formation, all four of which have had their underwing serials replaced by the legend 'Royal Navy'. Newark Air Museum

Number 800 Squadron participated in The Paris Air Show at Le Bourget in June 1961 and were known as 'The Red Blades'. These two detailed photographs were taken during the previous month as the Squadron prepared for their later performances: Lt M K Johnson is seen inspecting and boarding his aircraft which had had smoke generating apparatus fitted into one of its jet pipes.
FAA Museum

Number 800 Squadron was disbanded at Lossiemouth on 25th February 1964, and its Scimitars were passed to No.803 Squadron. The squadron did not remain dormant for long and reformed on Buccaneers less than a month later.

No.804 Squadron

The last squadron to become operational with the Scimitar was No.804, which re-formed at Lossiemouth on 1st March 1960 with Lt Cdr T V G Binney as commanding officer. Following an intense period of work-up, detachments to HMS *Hermes* commenced in May for deck landing practice. The work-up was completed by 6th July and the squadron embarked on *Hermes* before sailing for the Mediterranean. It reached Malta on 11th July, with a visit to Messina from 22nd to 25th July, and then back to Malta for the 29th. The carrier visited Algeria on 18th August, before sailing home on the 22nd and arriving back at Rosyth on 5th September. The carrier sailed once more on the 15th to participate in a NATO exercise off the coast of Norway from the 21st. The second stage of this exercise took place from the 26th through to the 29th. Returning home the squadron stayed ashore until 28th November, when they flew to RAF North Front, Gibraltar, to rejoin *Hermes*. After an exercise in the Malta area the carrier sailed via Suez arriving at Aden on the 8th, and went on to spend Christmas Day at Colombo, Ceylon. The following day *Hermes* continued its journey arriving at Singapore on the 31st.

On 12th January 1961 *Hermes* departed for Subic Bay in the Philippines, arriving there on the 18th. It remained in the area until the 20th, then moved off to Hong Kong, arriving there on the 23rd. The carrier left again on the 1st February and arrived back at Singapore for maintenance on the 7th, before heading for home on the 18th. A stop was made at Trincomalee from the 24th to 27th, with participation in an exercise from then until the 9th March before arriving at Aden on the 17th and Malta on the 27th. Trials over the LABS Filfla Ranges were undertaken before the carrier departed on the 4th, visiting Naples on the 8th and then moving on to Gibraltar where it docked on the 12th. From there the carrier set course for home and arrived back at Portsmouth on 18th April, where the squadron flew off and headed back to Lossiemouth. They once again rejoined *Hermes* on 29th May for exercises in the English Channel, where the squadron achieved its 1,000th carrier landing on the 4th June. The carrier visited Falmouth on the 10th, then headed for the Lossiemouth area, arriving there on the 17th. Departing once again for exercises on the 19th, the carrier was back to Portsmouth by the 22nd and heading for NAS Norfolk, Virginia, USA on the 30th when events in the Middle East led to her being ordered to Gibraltar. Having reached the Rock on the 4th July, the situation in Kuwait proved not to require *Hermes'* presence, and so the carrier headed back to Portsmouth on the 21st, arriving on the 24th. The carrier and squadron took part in an exercise during the end of July and on the 15th *Hermes* visited Oslo for a four day tour, before returning to Portsmouth on the 25th. The squadron disembarked from *Hermes* for the last time on 10th September 1961, for a non-stop flight back to their base at Lossiemouth. On the 15th the squadron was disbanded, not having suffered any losses in either men or machines throughout its 18 month commission.

No.800B Squadron

This unit was formed at Lossiemouth on 9th September 1964 as a special unit, associated with but separate from No.800 Squadron. Number 800B's role was to investigate and develop the operational techniques of air-to-air refuelling particularly in respect of the underpowered Buccaneer S.1, with which No.800 Squadron was equipped. In certain conditions the S.1 could not be catapulted with a full weapons load *and* a full fuel load. Number 800B extended the operating range of the Buccaneer S.1, until its successor the S.2 entered service and overcame this limitation by developing almost 60% more thrust. The introduction of the S.2 eventually rendered No.800Bs role redundant. Number 800B could also refuel other suitably equipped aircraft types. This unit, although nominally established with a complement of four Scimitars, is known to have had as many as 14 allocated to it at various times during its short existence, although only four were normally embarked on a carrier at any one time. The Scimitar, when performing the air-to-air refuelling role, was equipped with a Mk.20A flight refuelling pod on the starboard inner pylon. The pod carried 145 gallons of fuel which could be replaced from the Scimitar's internal fuel supply as required. Despite being dedicated to the refuelling role the Scimitar's designation remained as F.1, a K suffix was never apparently applied. The unit embarked HMS *Eagle* on 2nd December 1964 and was the only aircraft carrier from which No.800B operated, excluding of course any cross-decking to other carriers. The unit spent a total of 17 months aboard *Eagle* or on detachment abroad prior to disbanding at Yeovilton on 14th August 1966.

Fleet Requirements Unit

One of the last uses of the type was not by the FAA, but by Airwork Limited, the Fleet Requirements Unit (FRU) based at Hurn Airport, near Bournemouth. Here 16 of the remaining Scimitars were allocated following the types withdrawal from frontline service. The civilian pilots of Airwork FRU were trained by No.764(B) Squadron. Airwork FRU undertook the task of simulated low-level attacks on naval shipping for defence exercises and training of air traffic controllers at RNAS Yeovilton. The Scimitar's involvement with these tasks came to an end at the close of 1970, and marked the last operational use of the Scimitar.

Final Service

The Scimitar's final role, albeit non-flying, was nonetheless of great importance. With the steady increase in the weight and speed of both military and civil aircraft there was an urgent need to conduct research into how such aircraft would behave on a slippery runway. To this end two Scimitars were used, the initial trials being undertaken by XD248, which was loaned to RAE Farnborough and undertook the tests during the first months of 1968. At the end of 1968 XD248 was replaced by XD219 and with the outer wing panels removed this airframe undertook 150 trials before it was written off on 9th January 1973. Its demise was spectacular, having missed the arrester wire on one run at over 120mph, it veered off the runway and hit a concrete plinth and was wrecked. The remains ended up as a crash rescue airframe at RNAS Yeovilton from 1990 before being finally sold as scrap in 1994.

All the Scimitars that remained when the type was declared obsolete were either scrapped or ended up at the Proof & Experimental Establishment at Shoeburyness, where they were used as gunnery targets. After Airwork FRU ceased using Scimitars most of their airframes ended up at Shoeburyness and by the late 1980s just a handful remained. These were either sold to a scrap dealer, or purchased by the MoD, who moved them to the Aberporth or Pendine ranges and used as targets. Today just three Scimitars remain intact.

Survivors

XD220 - After service use this airframe moved to the FAA Museum, Yeovilton where it was put in external store during 1970. It remained here until the mid-1980s when it was swapped for an ex-USMC F-4 Phantom and moved to the USS *Intrepid* Air and Space Museum, New York, where it remains today.

XD317 - Once it ended its service career with Airwork FRU at Hurn this airframe was delivered to the FAA Museum in August 1969. The airframe was moved into the 'Flightdeck' interactive display in the late 1990s and remains there to this day

XD332 - Now resides with the Solent Sky Exhibition, Southampton.

THE SCIMITAR IN RETROSPECT

Unlike its predecessor the Attacker, the Scimitar is viewed in retrospect as a successful design, albeit one that never achieved its full potential and which needs to be considered in light of the political, economic and military situation of its day.

By the time the Type 525 was flying in the early 1950s, Britain was still suffering from the effects of a lax attitude concerning research and development within the military aeronautical arena; one that had existed since the immediate post-war period. As a result, aircraft manufacturers were looking elsewhere for growth markets; particularly towards guided weapons and civil aircraft design. At the end of Second World War the government had had no option but to examine methods of reducing spending on the military which eventually culminated in the notorious Duncan Sandys 1957 Defence White Paper and its claim that the days of the 'manned interceptor' were over. Military planners were forced to accept less and less funding which led in turn to a massive reduction in men and machines, tempered by the certain knowledge that Russia had gleaned a great deal of technical data from Germany at the end of World War Two.

The arrival of the Soviet MiG-15 was a shock, as too were their massive jet bombers that flew above the operational altitude of current RAF interceptors. In Britain, this resulted in military aircraft development splitting, with one line of thought directed towards unmanned missiles as a form of interception, whilst others considered powerful manned jet aircraft to be the way forward. The Royal Navy was left with the certain knowledge that designs such as the Attacker and Sea Hawk which had ushered them into the jet age, were just not sufficiently advanced enough to succeed in a modern conflict. They needed a swept-wing design, although many high-ranking officers felt that there were too many unknown factors in relation to the operation of such a type from an aircraft carrier for such to be used. As related, the development and operational acceptance of the Scimitar was protracted and the type did not enter operational service until 1958, some four years after the first true (Type 525) prototype flew. By today's standards that is not long, but in the immediate post-war period, it was. Thankfully, much of the development work carried out by the RAE and Royal Navy in accepting the Attacker into service had paved the way for the Scimitar and included safer jet handling aboard ship and safer recovery systems whilst landing, making jet operations on carriers much less hazardous. (See this publisher's title *'Attacker – The Royal Navy's First Operational Jet Fighter'* particularly pages 8-9). However the combination of the speed offered by a swept-wing design and the need for a slow approach to land on a carrier were, at this stage, mutually incompatible from a design point of view. Diverting airflow and slowing the aircraft while retaining lift was difficult to overcome

and when combined with the new phenomenon of pitch-up associated with high-speed aircraft, it is no surprise that the Scimitar took both designers and pilots beyond what was then 'known'. To develop an understanding of such phenomena takes time, but to try and overcome this while simultaneously bringing a design into service use is not possible. Vickers-Supermarine was pushing the envelope, not just in aeronautic development but also in the speed in which they were trying to incorporate such knowledge into an existing design. As this book recounts, much time was spent in rectifying problems that were usually brought about by the understanding of a phenomenon and its cause; cause and effect meant that once one problem was overcome it usually brought about another and so on. Vickers-Supermarine had their work cut out trying to solve all of these while still meeting the ever-changing demands of government and military planners.

This latter point shares a common thread within the history of any aircraft design of the late 1940s and early 1950s. As the political and military world changed day by day, so those who conducted military planning were forced to react and change their minds too. To a certain extent this remains true today, but forward planning and a greater understanding of what is possible from an aerodynamic point of view means that the evolution of an existing design is the norm, with great leaps in airframe design only being undertaken through a long period of research and development.

The financial constraints of the immediate postwar period were at odds with the ever-changing nature of the perceived threat and, when combined with the rapid development of electronic equipment and jet engines, it is possible to see why many aircraft developed between 1946 and 1959, are today often considered to be also-rans or stop-gap designs. That the Scimitar ever saw service adoption amidst such a changing world is testament to all at Vickers-Supermarine, the RAE and Royal Navy, but by the late 1950s, it was obvious that a single-seat aircraft was not ideal for a strike aircraft. The huge demands placed on a pilot by the new range of electronic weapons systems meant it was no longer possible for him to fly and operate these at the same time. The Scimitar never reached its intended high or low-altitude speeds and was only very nearly supersonic in level flight. For an interceptor/fighter this was inadequate, which is probably why the Scimitar was soon relegated to the low-level strike role and the interceptor task assumed by the Sea Vixen even though the Scimitar retained its four 30mm cannon throughout its service life.(See this publisher's title 'Sea Vixen – De Havilland's Ultimate Fighter Aircraft'). Its bombing role was subsequently acquired by the Blackburn Buccaneer S.1, designed from the outset as a two-seater. On the whole the Scimitar was liked by those who flew it, both operationally and for trials, although it was not particularly well liked by the crews that serviced it as it was a complex aircraft that required a lot of maintenance. One pilot recounted that the aircraft spent more time being serviced than flown! The ground crew found maintaining the type a chore, it was an over-complex type in comparison with the relatively simple piston and jet-powered machines that had preceded it and the ever-present hydraulic problems were tedious to deal with. By the standards of the 1970s it was a large aircraft and nowhere near as 'user friendly' as current warplanes. That said, the design was at its limit even before it entered service and many ex-pilots have commented that the type was barely an improvement on Second World War technology for a fighter. New navigational and attack systems however would have required a major redesign. The American's who saw and flew the Scimitar probably summed up its main failing when they said that, ''…only the British could build an aircraft with all that power and still remain sub-sonic''! The Scimitar could have been developed further, but, as the two-seat Sea Vixen had taken over the interceptor role and possessed full all-weather interception capability and with the Blackburn Buccaneer nearing service entry, there was simply little need to develop it further. The Scimitar had played its part and proved that a high-speed swept-wing aircraft could operate from a carrier, although, its lack of development means that history will always see the Scimitar as an interim design.

Opposite top: F.1 XD274 No.803 Squadron 024/E, May 1966. XD274 had been transferred earlier that month from No.800B Squadron and retained for a time the tankard image from the latter unit. The letter 'E' has been suitably modified to read 'E'mpty. Brian Lowe

Opposite bottom: F.1 XD243 025/E. Whilst still retaining the foaming tankard image on its fin from its previous unit, XD243 had been transferred to No.803 Squadron on 6th May 1966. Newark Air Museum

Opposite top: *F.1 145/V and a close-up view of No.803 Squadron's Badge, often applied prior to the Squadron's later adoption of a chequered pattern on the Scimitar's tail fin.* FAA Museum

Above: *No.803 Squadron formation fly past.* Brian Lowe

Opposite bottom: *F.1s XD244 151/H (HMS Hermes), XD213 152/H, 147/H and 150/H. From April 1962 No.803 Squadron adopted a yellow and black chequered pattern on their tail fins with the letter 'H' (later 'R') in white. Beyond the four Scimitars sit a number of Sea Vixens, Firestreak-equipped Gloster Javelins and a Bristol Britannia.* Brian Lowe

Above: *The forward deck park of (presumably) HMS* Hermes *as all of the Scimitars and Sea Vixens visible carry the letter 'H' on their tails. XD333 was the last Scimitar to be completed, (XD334 to XD357 having been cancelled) and was first flown on 22nd December 1960 with its final flight occurring on 20th January 1971.* Brian Lowe

following August. Note that one of the two Scimitars has a black nose cap. The Buccaneer 107/E is from No.800 Squadron, which had re-equipped with this type from March 1964. Various helicopters and an Avro Anson sit in the background. Authors collection

Below: *F.1 XD225 154/R No.803 Squadron in mid-1964. The letter 'H' had been replaced by 'R' in May 1964 when the Squadron joined HMS* Ark Royal *and XD225's individual code was changed to 147/R the*

Opposite: *Scimitars of No.804 Squadron overfly Farnborough in 1961. A line of English Electric Lightnings can be seen below, attended by ground crew in gleaming white overalls.* FAA Museum

Above: *Number 807 Squadron on parade at Lossiemouth. From left to right the aircraft are XD267 193/R, XD250 197/R, XD268 194/R, XD243 190/R and XD249196/R. Author's collection*

Below: *F.1 XD321 161/H, No.804 Squadron, 1960, location not stated although it is possibly Lossiemouth, the Squadron's shore base. Number 804 Squadron reformed with the Scimitar in March 1960, it was* allocated the codes 161 to 166 inclusive and featured a white tail fin with tiger head and sword Motif superimposed, along with the letter 'H'. The number '5' below the Scimitar's rear fuselage belongs to another aircraft, presumably 165/H. Of note is the row of Hawker Sea Furies beyond XD321's nose. No.804 Squadron used the Scimitar for just 18 months and was disbanded in September 1961. FAA Museum*

Above: Trained by the personnel of No.764B Squadron, several pilots employed by Airwork Limited continued to fly the Scimitar for a few years after the aircraft had ceased flying with the Fleet Air Arm. Based at Hurn, the Fleet Requirements Unit undertook a number of tasks on behalf of the Royal Navy. The FRU was initially allocated codes for the Scimitar from 025 to 038, later changed to 830 to 839. Scimitar 835 seen here, is XD267 which flew for the last time in 1969. FAA Museum

Below: F.1 XD219 at RAE Farnborough. This aircraft was last flown on 16th December 1968 when it was transferred to Ministry of Technology charge at Farnborough and struck off charge by the Royal Navy. Thereafter, with wings cropped, the aircraft was used for a series of wet runway and aquaplaning trials as seen here. On 9th January 1973 its participation in these trials came to an untimely end when its back was broken following a high speed run and collision with a set of runway landing lights. FAA Museum

Chapter 5: **TECHNICAL DESCRIPTION AND ARMAMENT**

The Scimitar F.1 was a single seat, twin-engine, jet-propelled fighter and long-range strike support day fighter. It was a low-wing, swept-back monoplane with a retractable tricycle undercarriage. Armed with four 30mm cannon it could, via simple modifications, undertake photo-reconnaissance and refuelling roles. The complete airframe description, is as follows.

Fuselage
The all-metal fuselage was of oval section except for the front and rear portions and was built up of frames, longerons, intercostals and light alloy plating. The front section accommodated the pilot in a pressurised cockpit with an electrically operated jettisonable sliding canopy and an ejection seat. Forward of the pressurised section the fuselage nose could be folded back. Immediately aft of the cockpit were Nos.1 and 2 fuel tanks, in tandem on the aircraft centreline, between the engine air intakes. The engine bays extended from frame 12 to 17 and were separated from each other by a vertical member on the aircraft centreline; the member incorporated a firewall. Aft of the engine bays the fuselage section changed to form housings for the jet pipes and, between the housings, fore-and-aft, were Nos.3, 4 and 5 fuel tanks. Hydraulically operated air brakes were provided. They comprised six small flaps (mounted three each side of the fuselage) installed, just forward of the jet pipe outlets, in the outboard skin structure of the jet pipe housing. The jet pipe outlets were at frame 25; aft of this point the fuselage became circular and at frame 29 merged with the empennage.

Wings
These were of all-metal construction with forward, main and aft spars and were swept back 45° at 25% chord. The mainplane had an aerofoil section at the fuselage of NACA 0008/64, an incidence of +1° and no dihedral. They were bolted to the fuselage through root end fittings. Hydraulically powered mainplane folding was provided. An integral fuel tank was built into each inner and outer portion of the mainplane; the skin plate in these areas was machined, heavy gauge material. Trailing edge flaps were fitted to the inner mainplanes; air, ducted from the engines, was blown over these flaps to augment lift. Fuselage flaps formed an extension of the trailing edge flaps. Leading edge flaps were fitted to both inner and outer mainplanes. A pressure head was fitted to the port mainplane tip.

Tail
The tailplane had an aerofoil section at the fuselage and tip of NACA 0007/64. Anhedral was 10° and the angle of sweep-back 40° at 25% chord. The empennage structure was built up to carry the swept-back fin, the tailplane and its hydraulic actuator, the tail bumper, deck arrester hook and hold-back gear. The tail bumper and deck arresting hook were retractable, with fixed fairings and doors to complete the contour. The fin sweep-back was 44.5° at 25% chord.

Undercarriage
The main undercarriage units were attached to the main spar of the inner mainplane and retracted into the fuselage. The nose undercarriage unit was attached to the forward portion of the fuselage at frames 7 and 9, and retracted into the fuselage.

Engines
The Scimitar was powered by two Rolls-Royce Avon Mk 202 straight-flow turbo-jet engines. Each engine was suspended at four points. Engine starting was by low pressure air motor. An air intake in the forward end of the dorsal fin provided cooling air for the engines and jet pipes. Three fire extinguisher bottles were installed, with a 'firewire' indication system in the engine bays and around the jet pipes.

Hydraulic System
These comprised two main systems, each independently powered by two engine-driven pumps (total of four) arranged so that each engine drove two pumps, connected one to each system. No.1 system operated the landing gear, tail bumper, deck arresting hook, wheel brakes, landing flaps, mainplane fold, air brakes, aileron control-run actuator and ailerons, tailplane and tailplane feel simulator, gun bay scavenge scoop and fuel flow proportioner. No.2 system operated the rudder and rudder feel simulator, aileron control-run actuator and ailerons, tailplane and tailplane feel simulator and the emergency hydraulic pump/motor unit. Two oil coolers were fitted, fuel being used as the cooling medium.

Flying Controls
These were hydraulically operated and were controlled by a conventional control column and rudder bar. The tailplane and ailerons were powered by dual hydraulic systems. The rudder, powered by one system only, reverted automatically to manual control should the associated hydraulic system fail. Hydraulic 'feel simulation' was provided for the tailplane and rudder controls, and spring 'feel' for the aileron con-

trol. Electrically operated trimming actuators were fitted into each control run. The tailplane was interconnected with the trailing edge flaps. Main wheel brake units were foot operated through the rudder bar.

Electrical System

This was a 28 volt d.c. single-pole earth-return installation powered by two 28 volt, 6 kilowatt engine driven wide-speed generators charging one 24 volt, 25 amp/hour battery. A conventional power supply control circuit was used for each generator. A.C. power for instruments was supplied by two 115 volt, 3-phase inverters which employed an automatic change-over circuit arrangement to provide stand-by facilities. A.C. power for the radar was obtained by the use of Type 200 and Type 108 inverters. Radio services included UHF communication and homing systems, telebreifing, altimeter and navigational and operational aids.

Radio & Radar Installation

UHF	ARI 18124/1
Standby UHF	ARI 23057
Homing UHF	ARI 18120
Radio Altimeter	ARI 5378
Navigational Aid	ARI 18107/1 [ARI 5885 post Mod.5012]
Radar Ranging Mk 1	ARI 5820
IFF Mk 10	ARI 5848

Fuel

Fuel was carried in five bag tanks in the fuselage and four integral tanks in the mainplanes. Provision was made for the carrying of four jettisonable fuel tanks fitted two port and two starboard, beneath the mainplane. The fuel system was pressurised and a balance system regulated the supply from individual internal tanks; a fuel proportioner controlled the supply from the jettisonable tanks. Two recuperators maintained a supply of fuel to the engines for a limited period when the aircraft was subjected to negative 'G'. In later aircraft, a refuelling-in-flight probe could be fitted, when required, to the fuselage nose.

The capacity of the fuel tanks was as follows:

No.1 (fuselage) tank	93	gallons
No.2 (fuselage) tank	253	"
Nos.3 and 4 (fuselage) tanks	170	"
No.5 (fuselage) tank	206	"
Port inner mainplane tank	61.5	"
Starboard inner mainplane tank	61.5	"
Port outer mainplane tank	103.5	"
Starboard outer mainplane tank	103.5	"
Recuperators	12	"
Total (internal)	**1,064**	"
Port inner jettisonable tank	200	"
Starboard inner jettisonable tank	200	"
Port outer jettisonable tank	200	"
Starboard outer jettisonable tank	200	"
Total fuel capacity (all tanks)	**1,864**	"

Armament

This comprised four 30mm ADEN guns mounted two each in gun bays, port and starboard underside of the fuselage. Ammunition tanks (160 rounds per gun) were located in the inboard ends of the inner mainplanes with access via the top surface. On firing, a scoop on the ventral fuselage opened pushing air into the bays to cool the guns and purge the bays of gases and debris. Spent ammunition cases were directed to a collecting tank situated between the gun bays in the forward fuselage.

The type could carry four 1,000lb free-fall bombs, carried one each on the underwing pylons. Trials were also conducted with two 2,000lb bombs, but was never used operationally. Unguided 3in rocket projectiles (RPs), carried in two tiers of three rockets on each of the four pylons and these could be fired singularly, in groups or, more usually, in 'ripple' bursts. Although often overlooked, the Scimitar could carry Matra 68mm rocket pods. Usually only two were carried, one on each outer pylon, and these could be fired in the same manner as the 3in unguided RPs (single, group or 'ripple').

ADEN Cannon

The 30mm ADEN cannon was developed from the 20mm MG 213C which had been produced in Germany during the Second World War. Initial work had been started by Mauser in 1943, but by the time the war ended just five had been completed and the weapon was captured by Allied forces. The MG 213C was a belt-fed, electrically-fired, pneumatically-charged weapon and its development post-war in the UK was instigated by the Ministry of Supply. This development took place at the Armament and Development Establishment at Enfield, hence ADEN (**A**rmament and **D**evelopment **E**stablishment at E**N**field). The original 20mm calibre was increased to 30mm and by reversing certain components within the weapon it could easily be changed from left to right-hand feed. The gun featured a rotary breech, with five chambers that rotated so that each chamber was brought into line with the barrel when in the 12 o'clock position. The weapon had a cyclic rate of 1,000rpm and could withstand 150 rounds being fired in a single burst without overheating.

Bullpup

The Scimitar was cleared to carry this American built air-to-ground guided missile in the early 1960s. It was controlled via a radio link and command-guided after launch by the pilot via a switch mounted on the port side of the cockpit. Control was very basic, with only up, down, left and right commands being able to be sent separately. The missile deployed two parasite flares after launch to aid the pilot in aiming the missile. Throughout the Bullpups flight, the launch aircraft had to maintain a steady level course. The missile weighed 570lb, of which 250lb was the warhead. The

Scimitar was cleared to carry four of these missiles, but it was more usual for two to be carried, one on each of the outer pylons, with drop tanks inboard. Launch could be undertaken at speeds up to Mach 0.95 and at an angle of up to 45°. Maximum speeds for carriage of the missile was Mach 1.1 with a maximum 5G rolling pullout, but the pilot was to avoid rapid rates of roll, lest the missile became detached!

Sidewinder

By the early 1960s, reliance soley on cannon armament was becoming obsolete and as the Scimitar had no radar, the FAA procured the American-built AIM-9 Sidewinder passive infra-red homing air-to-air missile. This missile was cleared for use with the Scimitar in 1963 and because it was already well tested it was simply integrated into the Scimitars armament

Red Beard

The Scimitar was the first FAA aircraft to be assigned to the nuclear strike role. Much secrecy surrounded the use of the *Red Beard* 25 kiloton nuclear weapon employed by the Scimitar, it being officially known as the Target Marker Bomb (TMB)! Deployment of the weapon was via the LABS system and in this mode the gunsight was removed as well as the four ADEN cannon, their associated ammunition feed, empty cartridge case ejector chutes and their blast tubes. Exact details concerning *Red Beard* remain classified, but it was quite a crude device, potentially it could explode on being accidentally dropped or bumped, so it was never cleared for use on carriers. The weapon was tested using XD218 and the final trials relating to this weapon were undertaken in this machine by Dave Morgan on 19th and 20th September 1963.

F.1 XD248 195/R, No.807 Squadron, in 1959 carrying 24 3in rocket projectiles, six per pylon. K Darling via author

Opposite: Three Scimitars of No.807 Squadron perform a near vertical dive. This Squadron reformed in October 1958 with Scimitars and were allocated the codes 190 to 198 inclusive and featured a scimitar on their tail fins. Brian Lowe

systems. Usually one was carried on each outer pylon and once the infra-red seeking head of the missile had obtained a 'lock' on its target, the pilot was warned that the weapon was ready by an audio 'growl' in his headphones. The missile was only launched after visual sighting of the target by the pilot and the weapon was detonated either by contact or proximity fuses. The weapon was effective in the latter mode some 30ft from the target and should it miss its intended target it would self-destruct 24 seconds after losing its infra-red 'lock'.

Operational deployment of the weapon remains classified but from photographs of dummy bombs fitted to squadron aircraft it can be seen that a single weapon was carried on the port inboard pylon with a drop tank on the starboard inner pylon.

Above: *F.1s XD328 153/V and 149/V, No.803 Squadron. XD328 is fitted with a Matra rocket pod on its outboard port pylon and is seen aboard* HMS Victorious *prior to April 1962. The ships identity is confirmed by the twin automatic 3in anti-aircraft gun mounting seen in the foreground. Only* Victorious, *alone out of RN operated aircraft carriers, mounted this weapon; six twin mounts in all.* Author's collection

Below: *F.1 XD328 144/R, No.803 Squadron at RAF Leuchars, Fife in September 1964. This aircraft is fitted with a dummy Red Beard nuclear free-fall bomb on its inboard port pylon, with a Sidewinder air-to-air missile outboard.* Author's collection

Above: *F.1 XD214 146/H, No.803 Squadron, carrying a Bullpup missile on its port outer pylon, outboard guns only and a camera nose.* Brian Lowe

Below: *This is the same aircraft as seen in the opposite photograph with the same weapons fit under its port wing. The outer starboard pylon mounts a Bullpup air-to-surface missile, whilst the inboard pylon carries an in-flight refuelling pod, the drogue for which is just discernible in the previous photograph.* FAA Museum

Access panels and doors.

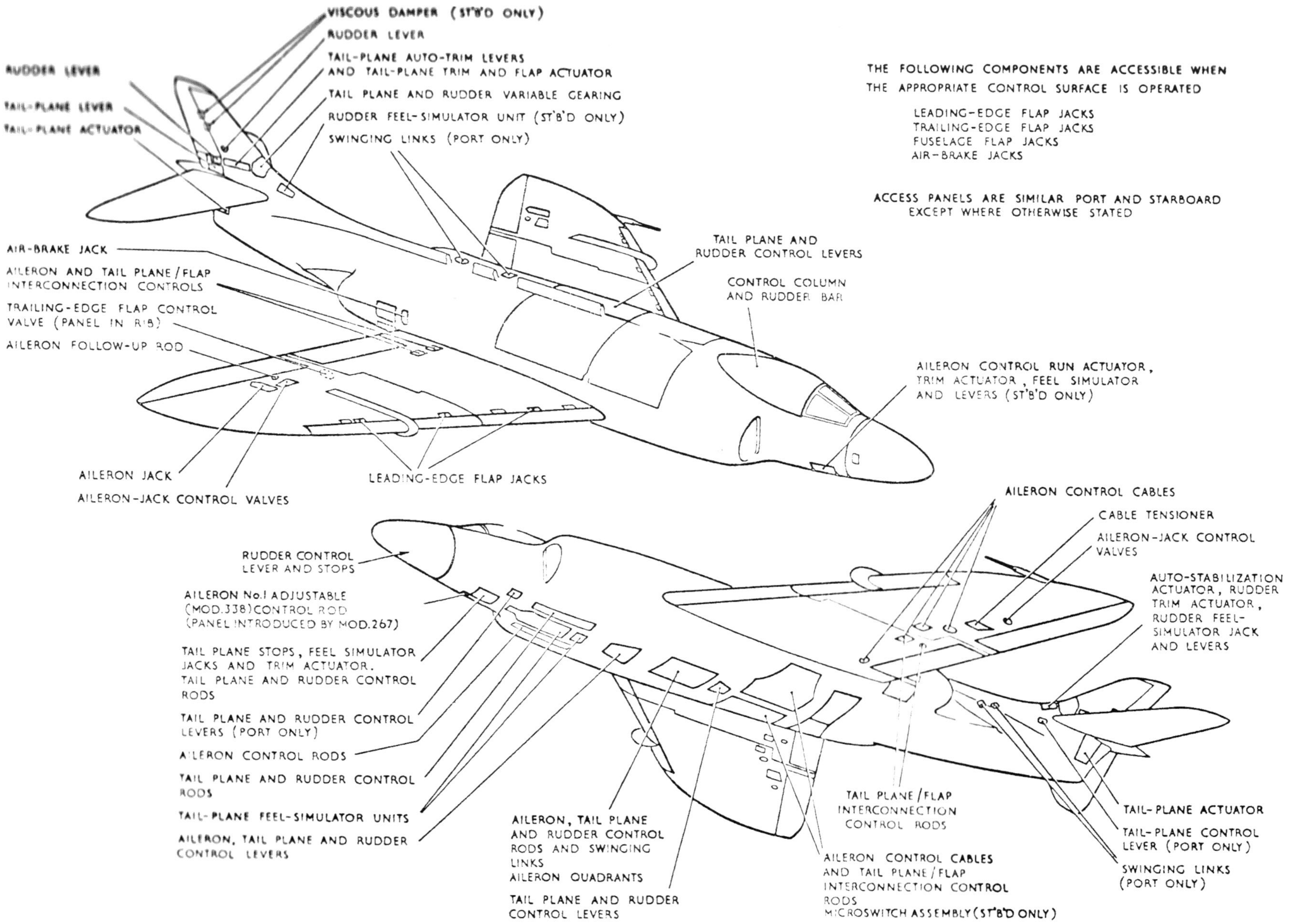

THE FOLLOWING COMPONENTS ARE ACCESSIBLE WHEN
THE APPROPRIATE CONTROL SURFACE IS OPERATED

LEADING-EDGE FLAP JACKS
TRAILING-EDGE FLAP JACKS
FUSELAGE FLAP JACKS
AIR-BRAKE JACKS

ACCESS PANELS ARE SIMILAR PORT AND STARBOARD
EXCEPT WHERE OTHERWISE STATED

AILERON CONTROL RUN ACTUATOR,
TRIM ACTUATOR, FEEL SIMULATOR
AND LEVERS (ST'B'D ONLY)

AILERON CONTROL CABLES

CABLE TENSIONER

AILERON-JACK CONTROL
VALVES

AUTO-STABILIZATION
ACTUATOR, RUDDER
TRIM ACTUATOR,
RUDDER FEEL-
SIMULATOR JACK
AND LEVERS

TAIL-PLANE ACTUATOR

TAIL-PLANE CONTROL
LEVER (PORT ONLY)

SWINGING LINKS
(PORT ONLY)

TAIL PLANE/FLAP
INTERCONNECTION
CONTROL RODS

AILERON CONTROL CABLES
AND TAIL PLANE/FLAP
INTERCONNECTION CONTROL
RODS
MICROSWITCH ASSEMBLY(ST'B'D ONLY)

TAIL PLANE AND
RUDDER CONTROL LEVERS

CONTROL COLUMN
AND RUDDER BAR

AILERON, TAIL PLANE
AND RUDDER CONTROL
RODS AND SWINGING
LINKS
AILERON QUADRANTS

TAIL PLANE AND RUDDER
CONTROL LEVERS

VISCOUS DAMPER (ST'B'D ONLY)

RUDDER LEVER

TAIL-PLANE AUTO-TRIM LEVERS
AND TAIL-PLANE TRIM AND FLAP ACTUATOR

TAIL PLANE AND RUDDER VARIABLE GEARING

RUDDER FEEL-SIMULATOR UNIT (ST'B'D ONLY)

SWINGING LINKS (PORT ONLY)

LEADING-EDGE FLAP JACKS

RUDDER LEVER

TAIL-PLANE LEVER

TAIL-PLANE ACTUATOR

AIR-BRAKE JACK

AILERON AND TAIL PLANE/FLAP
INTERCONNECTION CONTROLS

TRAILING-EDGE FLAP CONTROL
VALVE (PANEL IN R.8.)

AILERON FOLLOW-UP ROD

AILERON JACK

AILERON-JACK CONTROL VALVES

RUDDER CONTROL
LEVER AND STOPS

AILERON No.1 ADJUSTABLE
(MOD.JJ81)CONTROL ROD
(PANEL INTRODUCED BY MOD.267)

TAIL PLANE STOPS, FEEL SIMULATOR
JACKS AND TRIM ACTUATOR.
TAIL PLANE AND RUDDER CONTROL
RODS

TAIL PLANE AND RUDDER CONTROL
LEVERS (PORT ONLY)

AILERON CONTROL RODS

TAIL PLANE AND RUDDER CONTROL
RODS

TAIL-PLANE FEEL-SIMULATOR UNITS

AILERON, TAIL PLANE AND RUDDER
CONTROL LEVERS

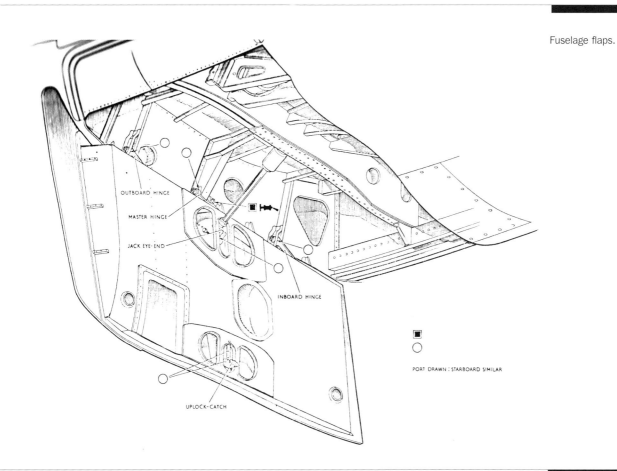

Fuselage flaps.

OUTBOARD HINGE

MASTER HINGE

JACK EYE-END

INBOARD HINGE

UPLOCK-CATCH

PORT DRAWN : STARBOARD SIMILAR

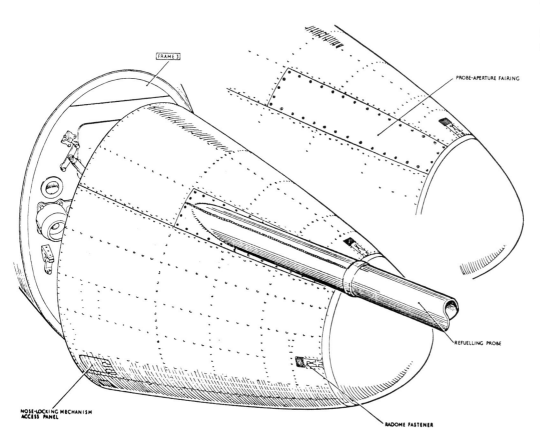

Forward nose with refuelling probe.

FRAME 3

PROBE-APERTURE FAIRING

REFUELLING PROBE

NOSE-LOCKING MECHANISM ACCESS PANEL

RADOME FASTENER

Jet pipe installation

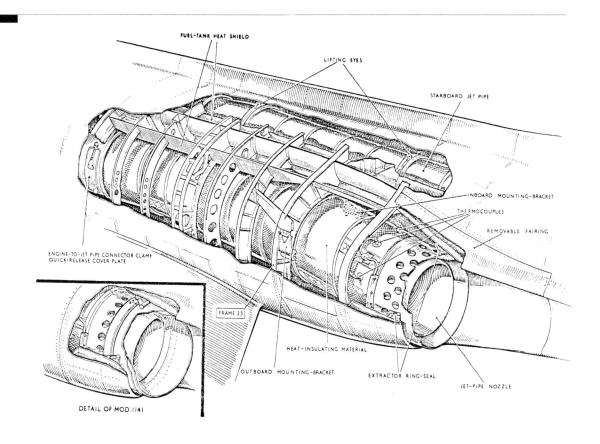

FUEL-TANK HEAT SHIELD

LIFTING EYES

STARBOARD JET PIPE

INBOARD MOUNTING-BRACKET

THERMOCOUPLES

REMOVABLE FAIRING

ENGINE-TO-JET PIPE CONNECTOR CLAMP
QUICK-RELEASE COVER PLATE

FRAME 23

HEAT-INSULATING MATERIAL

OUTBOARD MOUNTING-BRACKET

EXTRACTOR RING-SEAL

JET-PIPE NOZZLE

DETAIL OF MOD.1141

Accelerator hooks

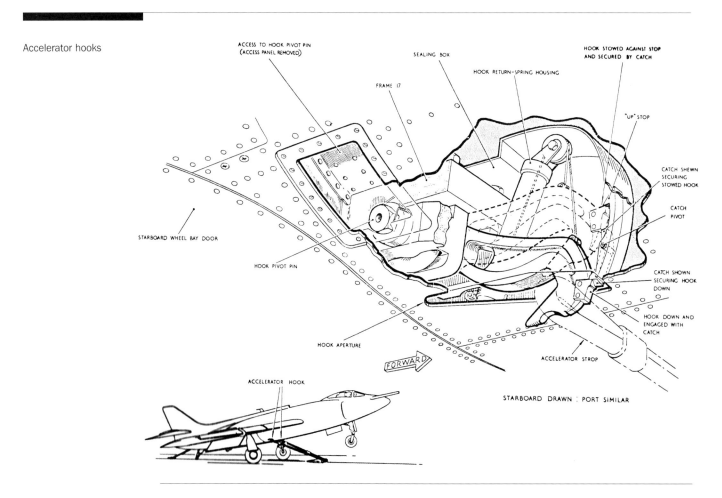

ACCESS TO HOOK PIVOT PIN
(ACCESS PANEL REMOVED)

SEALING BOX

HOOK STOWED AGAINST STOP
AND SECURED BY CATCH

HOOK RETURN-SPRING HOUSING

FRAME 17

"UP" STOP

CATCH SHEWN
SECURING
STOWED HOOK

CATCH
PIVOT

STARBOARD WHEEL BAY DOOR

HOOK PIVOT PIN

CATCH SHOWN
SECURING HOOK
DOWN

HOOK DOWN AND
ENGAGED WITH
CATCH

HOOK APERTURE

FORWARD

ACCELERATOR STROP

STARBOARD DRAWN : PORT SIMILAR

ACCELERATOR HOOK

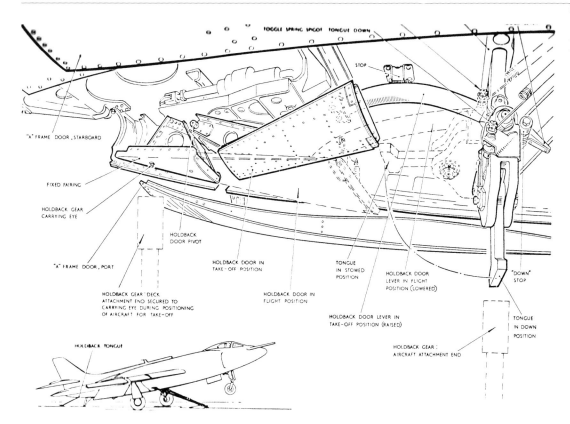

Accelerator holdback torque.

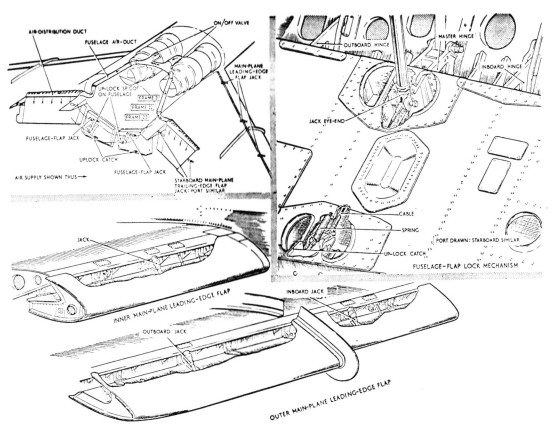

Arrangement of flaps and blown-flap ducting.

Main undercarriage
assembly.

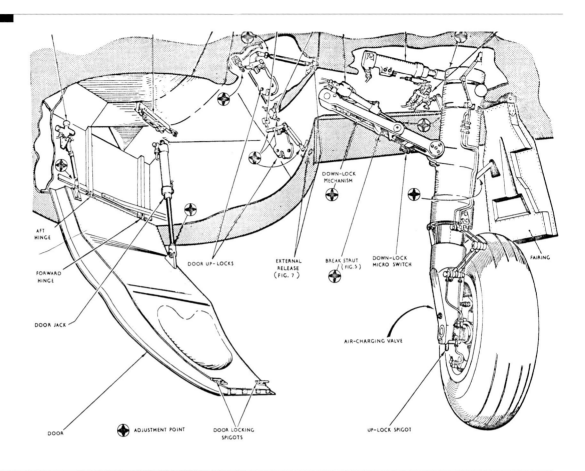

Nose undercarriage
assembly.

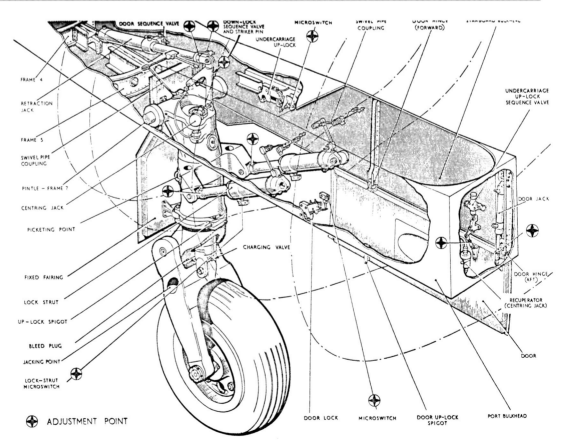

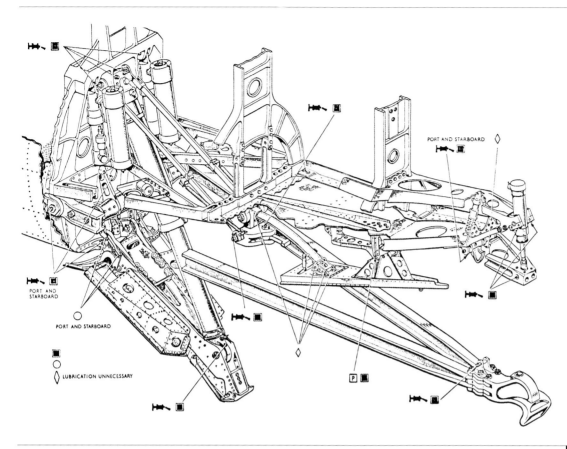

Tail bumper and deck arresting gear.

LUBRICATION UNNECESSARY

PORT AND STARBOARD

PORT AND STARBOARD

PORT AND STARBOARD

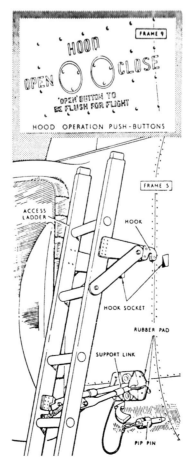

Cockpit access.

HOOD
OPEN   CLOSE
'OPEN' BUTTON TO BE FLUSH FOR FLIGHT
HOOD OPERATION PUSH-BUTTONS

FRAME 9

FRAME 5

ACCESS LADDER

HOOK

HOOK SOCKET

RUBBER PAD

SUPPORT LINK

PIP PIN

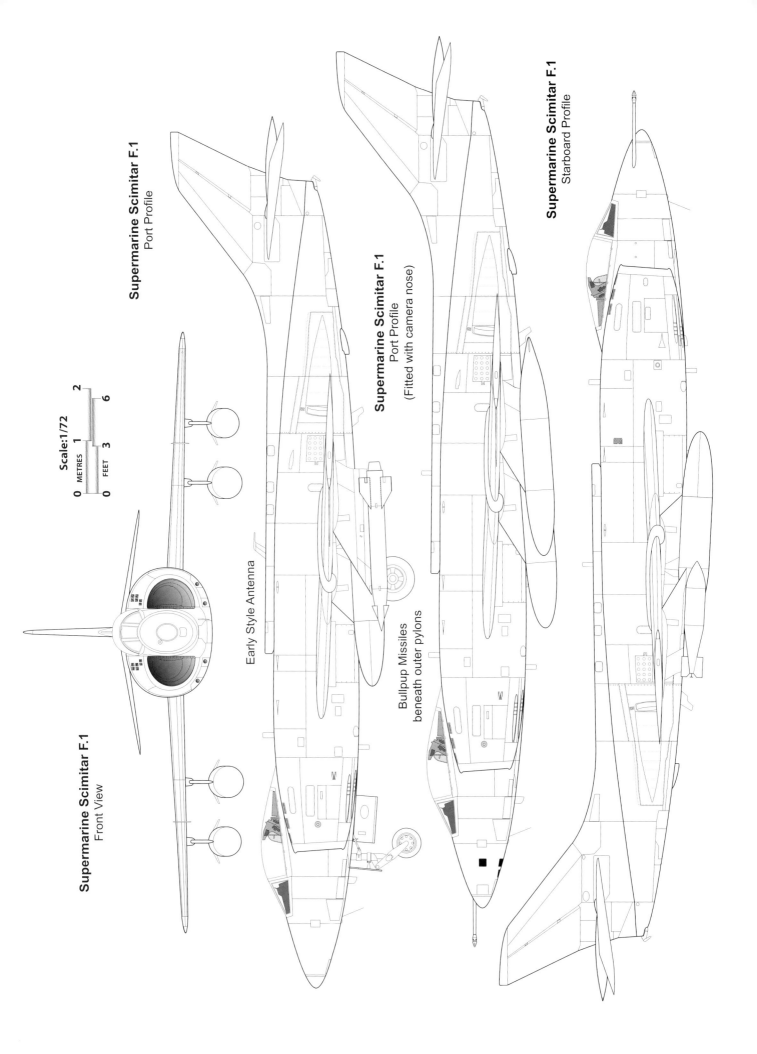

Supermarine Scimitar F.1
Port Profile

Supermarine Scimitar F.1
Port Profile
(Fitted with camera nose)

Supermarine Scimitar F.1
Starboard Profile

Supermarine Scimitar F.1
Front View

Scale:1/72

METRES 0   1   2

FEET   0   3   6

Early Style Antenna

Bullpup Missiles
beneath outer pylons

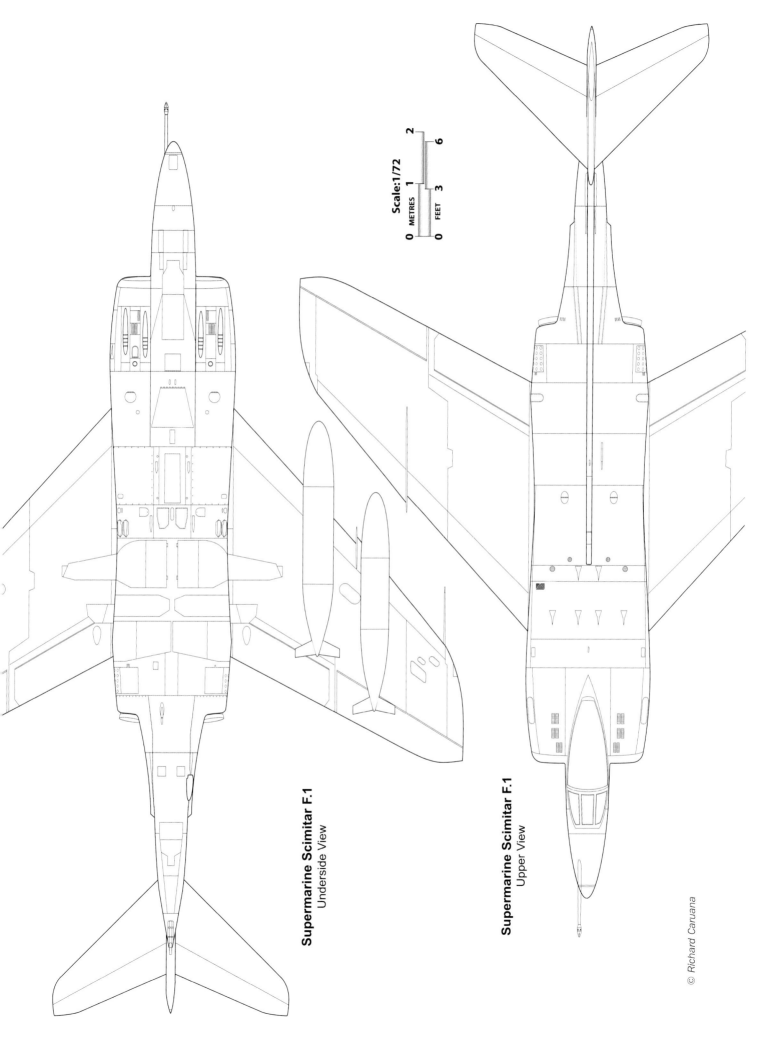

Scale:1/72

Supermarine Scimitar F.1
Underside View

Supermarine Scimitar F.1
Upper View

Chapter 6: SCIMITAR COLOURS

For the majority of its service life the Scimitar wore a standard scheme, although there were exceptions.

Type 508

Throughout the whole of its career VX133 remained unpainted. It had roundels applied above and below the wings and on either side of the fuselage. These were type D roundels of 32in diameter. (Please note that when the mock-up of the Type 508 was viewed it featured, then current, type C1 roundels on the fuselage and none on the wings). Initially VX133 carried its serial on either side of the aft fuselage, just under the trailing edge of the tailplanes, in 8in black characters. The 508 never carried, as far as is known, the 'Royal Navy' legend on the aft fuselage at any time during its life. The serial number was repeated in 28in black characters under each wing, with those under the port orientated to be read from the front and those under the starboard, from the rear. Ejection seat warning triangles in red were applied each side of the nose, directly in line with the pilot's seat, about mid-way down the fuselage sides.

Type 529

The Type 529, VX136, was similar in many ways to the Type 508 and remained unpainted throughout its career. Studying photographs however, it seems that the extreme tip of the nose was a white or cream colour and it is presumed this area was not metal (fibreglass maybe?). 28in diameter type D roundels and 8in black serial numbers were applied to the fuselage, with 32in type D roundels on the upper and lower wings and the serial number repeated under each wing in the same manner as those on the Type 508. Unlike the Type 508 it did carry the 'Royal Navy' legend on each side of the rear fuselage, it was applied below the serial number VX136.

Type 525

When first rolled out VX138 was unpainted. It featured Type D roundels on the rear fuselage, albeit a little higher than on the previous two aircraft. The roundels were again repeated above and below the wings, although the lower ones were further outboard, within about 2ft of the tip. The swept wing also meant that although the orientation of the serial under each wing remained, its alignment changed so that it was in line with the trailing edge. As the trailing edge was at a different angle, when viewed from underneath, the serials seemed to be 'mis-aligned', but they were not. From the beginning this airframe carried both the serial and Royal Navy legend, written as one line (Royal Navy VX138), with these handed so that text on each

side read from left to right. By the time this aircraft appeared at the SBAC event at Farnborough in September 1954 it had been painted 'cream' overall. As far as can be determined there is no official record as to the precise mix for this shade. By the time VX138 was cream overall it had acquired the red ejection seat warning triangles, although these were applied high up on each side of the cockpit area, just below and slightly forward of the top of each intake. The aircraft also had a number of warning stencils applied in black, these can be seen on contemporary images, although their wording is unknown. By mid-1955 the airframe had acquired an FAA colour scheme of Extra Dark Sea Grey (some state it to be Dark Sea Grey, but that was contrary to the official regulations of the era) upper surfaces and Sky underneath. The demarcation was very high on the fuselage dorsal spine, with the vertical fin and rudder in Sky, the norm for FAA machines of this era. The upper surface colour on the wing and tailplane wrapped round the leading edges by 6in onto the lower surfaces. Very few images exist of the aircraft in this scheme, as it was destroyed on 5th July 1955. From the study of available images it seems that the aircraft had acquired Type D roundels of a much larger diameter (36in?) on the rear fuselage and, possibly on the wings. The serial number appears to be missing from the aft fuselage, but the 'Royal Navy' legend was applied in very large characters. No clear images have been found of the underside of the aircraft in this scheme, so we can only speculate that the type had the larger Type D roundels under each wing and retained the serial numbers as per the previous two prototypes?

Type 544

WT854, was delivered in the FAA scheme of Extra Dark Sea Grey (BS640) over Sky. The demarcation was now in line with the wings leading and trailing edges. This meant that the entire vertical fin and dorsal spine were now also grey. The roundel was applied to the fuselage sides just forward of the main wing leading edge. These roundels seem to be of the same size as seen on the Type 525 (36in?) and 529, but those on the upper and lower wings are smaller. The upper ones seem to be positioned at a point mid-way between the wing tip and wing fence, while those underneath are nearly at the tip, with the outer arc clipping the projection of the upper surface colour. As already mentioned the upper surface colour wraps around the leading edge and projects aft. Serial numbers were applied in black 8in characters on the rear fuselage, mid-way along the exhaust plates. The 'Royal Navy' legend on WT854 comprised larger and broader characters than the serial number and was placed on the vertical fin fillet, orientated to read from right to left on both sides. The second Type 544, WT859, was finished in the same scheme as WT854, although it did not initially have the prominent pitot tube installed in the nose.

The third Type 544, WW134 was more representative of production aircraft and consequently seems to have carried more stencilling making it similar to the Scimitars that would follow. All of the colour and marking comments made for WT854 and WT859 apply to WW134 also. By the time WW134 was used for trials in the Mediterranean in 1962 she was in a sorry state, with a rudimentary fake nose cone fitted, the intake lips were painted yellow on the top half and black on the bottom. The nose seems to have the lower section, below the demarcation painted black(?), while the upper section of the replacement nose cone seems to be a light shade, that is probably not white, so may well be yellow.

Service Scimitars

In service the Scimitar only carried one scheme throughout its life. This scheme was similar to the overall one seen on the Type 544s, with Extra Dark Sea Grey on the upper surfaces. The Sky on the lower surfaces of the prototypes was replaced with white. The position, style and colour of the roundels and serial numbers remained the same as the Type 544. The only difference with these service machines was the application of squadron codes and insignia as described in the following squadron summaries. Each aircraft carrier was allocated a code letter which was also applied to the vertical fin of the majority of aircraft embarked upon it, or allocated to it. Most naval air bases also used codes, RNAS Ford was 'FD', Lossiemouth 'LM', Yeovilton 'VL', whilst HMS *Ark Royal* was 'R', HMS *Centaur* 'C', HMS *Eagle* 'E', HMS *Hermes* 'H' and HMS *Victorious* 'V'.

No.700 Squadron

This unit applied codes in the 510-512 range in black on a white rectangle on either side of the nose. The last two digits of this was repeated in black on the nose-wheel door. The base code for RNAS Ford – FD was applied in white to either side of the vertical fin. This base code was changed to VL in September 1958 when the unit moved to Yeovilton

No.700X Squadron

This unit applied codes in the 800-806 range placed directly to either side of the nose in a variety of styles. The base code FD was applied to both sides of the vertical fin.

No.736 Squadron

This unit applied codes in the 608-618 range initially in white on a black nose panel. The last two digits were repeated in black on the nose-wheel door and the base code LM was applied in black on either side of the vertical fin. By September 1960 the codes changed to white on a dark grey panel, with the panel itself sometimes outlined in white and the LM code applied in white. By 1961 the LM code on the fin had been replaced with a blue lightning flash on a white background.

No.764 Squadron

Apparently codes were not applied to Scimitars during their short period of service with No.764 Squadron.

No.764B Squadron

This unit allocated codes in the 614-617 and 620-621 ranges. These were applied above the wings, on the mid-fuselage, in white. As the machines operated by this squadron came from No.736 squadron, they retained the blue lightning flash on the white vertical fin.

No.800 Squadron

This unit allocated codes in the 100-113 range and these were painted in black characters outlined in white. The last digit of these codes were applied in black to the nose-wheel door and in white to the upper surface of the inboard flaps. The carrier code R (HMS *Ark Royal*) was applied in white to each side of a red vertical fin.

No.800B Flight

This unit allocated codes in the 111-117 range. These codes were applied in white, mid-fuselage, above the wing. The carrier code E (HMS *Eagle*) was painted in white on the vertical fin. The unit's association with the Whitbread Brewery led to the adoption of a tankard emblem on either side of the vertical fin, this was yellow with white foam and details.

No.803 Squadron

The unit codes were initially in the 143-159 range. These were applied to either side of the nose in yellow or gold thinly outlined in black. The carrier code V was in white on the vertical fin and some machines carried a unit badge pierced by a yellow and black chequered arrowhead on the forward engine cowling. The codes later moved to the mid-fuselage, above the wings, applied in white and repeated in black on the nose-wheel door. From April 1962 the unit badge was deleted and black and yellow checks were applied to the vertical fin, with a small 'H' in the bottom right hand black check. This was replaced in May 1964 by the letter R, and from July 1965 the aircraft code numbers changed to 015-017, 020-027 and 030-034.

No.804 Squadron

This unit applied codes in the 161-166 range. These were black outlined in white on the nose, with the last digit in black on the nose-wheel door. The vertical fin

Below: *XV138 resplendent in its overall cream scheme is seen taxiing in after landing at the 1954 SBAC show at Farnborough. Barry Jones*

Bottom: *F.1 XD215 611/FM, 'No.736 Squadron', (in reality No.764B Squadron), at Biggin Hill Air Fair, 14th May 1965. See chapter 4 page 30 for further details. XD215 appears to have suffered significant damage to its rudder, although it would seem that the latter has been turned to its extreme right whilst the 'torn' effect is created by a dark blue flag drooping from the flag pole in the distance.* Newark Air Museum

was white, superimposed with the squadron's tiger motif. The carrier code H was applied in black at the top of the vertical fin.

No.807 Squadron

Codes were allocated in the 190-198 range. These were initially either in bronze or light blue, outlined in black on either side of the nose with the last digit repeated on the nose-wheel door in black. The codes later changed however and appeared in black often edged in white. The carrier code R was applied in white on the vertical fin with the squadron scimitar motif. In March 1961 the carrier code changed to C.

In many instances the Scimitar had the extreme tip of its nose cone painted black from an unknown date.

Secondline Service

The only organisations to operate the Scimitar outside of the FAA were various MoD establishments as well as Airwork Limited at Hurn. The latter applied codes initially from 025 to 038, changing in December 1969 from 830 to 839. All machines used by Airwork

within the Fleet Requirements Unit were ex-squadron aircraft, and all retained their overall service scheme.

The only Scimitar to appear in a non-standard scheme other than prototypes was XD229. This machine was operated by the RAE Weapons Flight at West Freugh during 1964-1965. Most sources list this machine as being 'light blue' and white with black details. Some sources identify the blue as being 'powder blue', but there is no official documentation to accurately identify the colour. The legend 'Royal Navy' was not applied, but the serial was in the usual positions, albeit in small 8in black characters on the fuselage. At a later stage, on either side of the nose in yellow or possibly white appeared the legend 'Royal Aircraft Establishment', probably in 8in characters.

Above: *F.1 112/R, No.800 Squadron. Date and location not known.*
Newark Air Museum

Below: *A Scimitar of No.800 Squadron landing aboard HMS* Ark Royal *in
the Indian Ocean in 1963. In fact the aircraft 'bolted', i.e. it missed the
wires and had to go around again. A Westland Whirlwind plane guard
hovers off the port quarter.* Courtesy of Duncan Adams via Pete
Woodbridge

Above: *F.1 XD270 107/E, No.800 Squadron, about to be released from the arresting wire aboard HMS* Ark Royal *in the Indian Ocean in 1963.* Courtesy Duncan Adams via Pete Woodbridge

Below and the following three pages: *The following photographs are a series of seven images of No.800B Squadron.* Pete Woodbridge

Above: *A crowded scene in 1966 aboard HMS* Eagle *with Scimitars sharing the deck with an AEW Fairey Gannet, Sea Vixen FAW.2s and Buccaneer S.1s. The nearest Scimitar is XD243 115/E of No.800B Squadron, however the furthest is XD244 026/R from No.803 Squadron, of which the black chequered markings on its tail have been 'zapped' with foaming tankards! Number 803 Squadron had incidentally received new fuselage codes in 1965 consisting of the groups 015 to 017, 020 to 027 and 030 to 034. Courtesy of Pete Woodbridge*

Left: *In fact, XD244 was on temporary loan from No.803 Squadron to No.800B and so, the latter unit added the necessary embellishments. Ultimately this aircraft went on to make the last ever flight of a Scimitar on 12th February 1971. Courtesy of Pete Woodbridge*

Opposite top: *XD244 026R readied for launching.*
Pete Woodbridge

Opposite bottom: *HMS* Eagle *anchored with its complement of aircraft displayed on deck. A Scimitar can be seen at the head of the angled deck.*
Pete Woodbridge

Above: *F.1 XD268 156/V (HMS* Victorious*). Reformed in June 1958, from a nucleus of No.700X Squadron, No.803 proved to be the longest lived of the front-line Scimitar units. Initially the Squadron codes were 143 to 159 inclusive, although these would change at a later date. This aircraft had participated in the Paris to London 'Daily Mail' Bleriot Anniversary Race on 15th July 1959. Flown by Commander I Martin, it set the fastest overall time for a single-seat aircraft of 43 minutes and 11 seconds. FAA Museum*

Below: *In September 1958 No.803 Squadron participated in formation displays at Farnborough. Standing in front of 147/V is the display team from left to right: Mike Maina, Lt Cdr Higgs, Lt Cdr Titford, Peter Barber, Cdr Russell (CO), John Beard and Ted Anson. 147/V displays the Squadron's initial marking pattern with the code positioned on the nose and (in some instances) a Squadron Badge surmounting a chequered arrow head. FAA Museum*

Above: *F.1 XD328 144/R, No.803 Squadron, Yeovilton, 28th August 1964. This is the same aircraft with the same underwing load as seen in chapter 5 at Leuchars during the following month.*
Newark Air Museum

Left: *Scimitar flypast at Yeovilton, 28th August 1964. The two aircraft closest to the camera are XD225 and XD278, whilst the third appears to be XD250. If so, this latter aircraft crashed into the Indian Ocean on 17th February 1966.*
Newark Air Museum

Right: *A selection of photographs showing No.803 Squadron Scimitars at Yeovilton on 28th August 1964.* Newark Air Museum

Opposite top: *An undated photograph of a Scimitar from No.807 Squadron.* FAA Museum

Opposite bottom: *F.1 038 from the FRU displaying an early code allocation which ran from 025 to 038 inclusive.* FAA Museum

Opposite top: *An undated photograph of a Scimitar from No.807 Squadron.* FAA Museum

Opposite bottom: *F.1 038 from the FRU displaying an early code allocation which ranged from 025 to 038 inclusive.* FAA Museum

Above: *HMS* Eagle *amidships. Just to the left of the 4.5in twin-gun turret and one deck below is a quad Seacat surface-to-air missile mounting.* Pete Woodbridge

Below: *Replenishment At Sea (RAS). A British warship's period at sea could and still is significantly extended by vessels of the Royal Fleet Auxiliary which have been specifically built or converted to carry everything that a warship and its crew require. Here an unidentified RFA replenishes* HMS Eagle *which has two Scimitars positioned at the deck edge.* Pete Woodbridge

Supermarine Type 544 WT854, January 1956.
Extra Dark Sea Grey/Sky finish with all lettering in black.

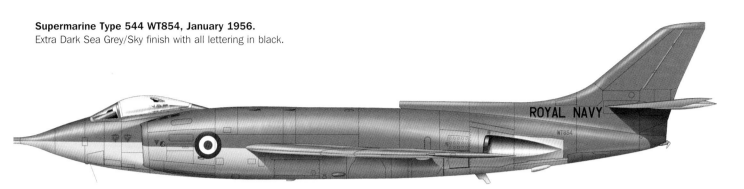

Supermarine Type 544 WT854, with modified (production) nose fitted.
Extra Dark Sea Grey/Sky finish with all lettering in black.

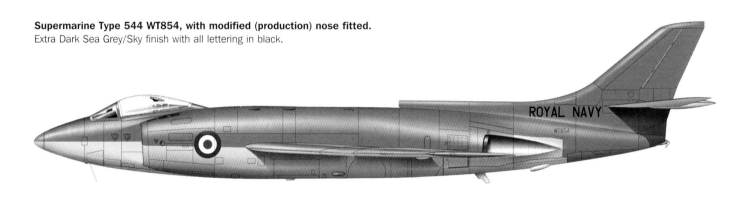

Scimitar F.1 XD220 800/FD No.700X Squadron, Scimitar Intensive Flying Unit, Ford, early 1958.
Extra Dark Sea Grey/White scheme with all lettering in black, except for code 'FD' on fin which is white; '0' in black on nose-wheel door.

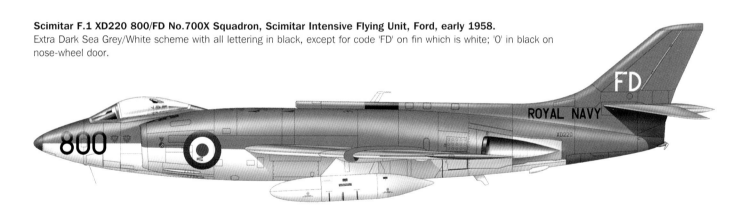

Scimitar F.1 XD221 801/FD No.700X Squadron, Scimitar Intensive Flying Unit, Ford.
Extra Dark Sea Grey/White scheme with all lettering in black, except for codes 'FD' and top half of '801' which are white; '1' in black on nose-wheel door.

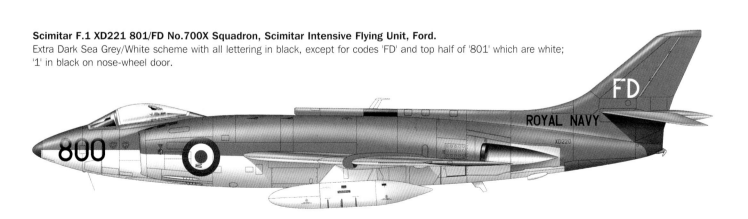

Scimitar F.1 XD230 805/FD, No.700X Squadron Intensive Flying Flight, Ford, March 1958.
Extra Dark Sea Grey/White scheme with lettering in black, except for codes 'FD' and top half of '805' which are in white; '5' in black on nose-wheel door.

Scimitar F.1 XD226 510/FD, No.700 Squadron, Ford, 1958.
Extra Dark Sea Grey/White scheme with lettering in black, except code 'FD' on fin which is white; '10' in black on nose-wheel door.

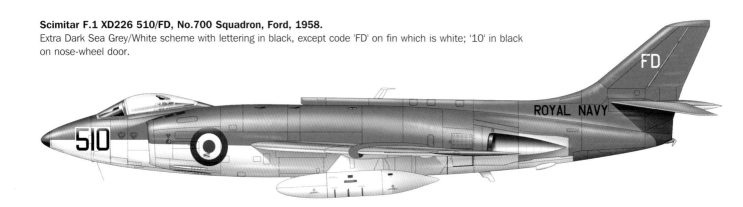

Scimitar F.1 XD220 511/VL, No.700 Squadron, Yeovilton, September 1958.
Extra Dark Sea Grey/White scheme with all lettering in black, except code 'VL' on fin which is white; '11' in black on nose-wheel door.

Scimitar F.1 XD239 613, No.736 Squadron, May 1962.
Extra Dark Sea Grey/White finish with white fin and blue lightning bolt superimposed; dark grey rectangle with white '613' on nose. RN legend and fuselage serial in white; serials below wings in black. '13' repeated in black on nose-wheel door.

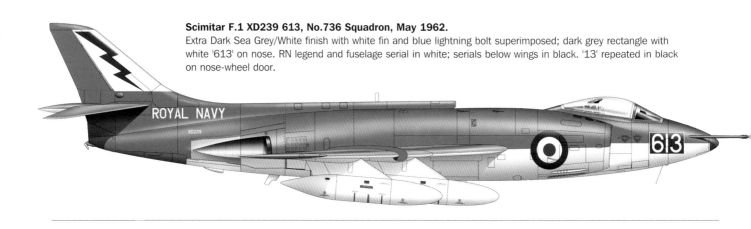

Scimitar F.1 XD224 614, No.736 Squadron, Lossiemouth, 1962.
Extra Dark Sea Grey/White finish with white fin and blue flash superimposed; white '614' on dark grey rectangle on nose, bordered in white. RN legend and serial in white; underwing serials and '14' on nose in black.

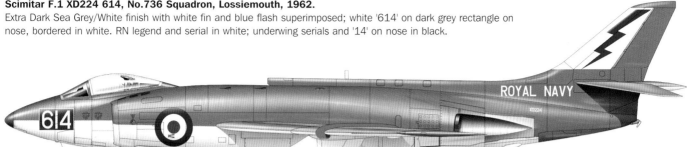

Scimitar F.1 XD215 614, No.736 Squadron, HMS *Hermes*.
Extra Dark Sea Grey/White scheme with white fin and blue lightning bolt in blue superimposed; white code '614', RN script and serial on fuselage. Underwing serials in black.

Scimitar F.1 XD230 617/LM, No.736 Squadron, Lossiemouth, 1960.
Extra Dark Sea Grey/White finish with lettering in black, except code 'LM' which is white; nose code is white on blue rectangle. The Squadron Badge was not carried on the starboard side.

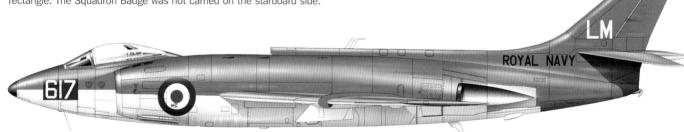

Scimitar F.1 XD322 106/R, No.800 Squadron, HMS *Ark Royal*, 1961.
Extra Dark Sea Grey/White finish with red fin and white code 'R'; '106' on nose in black, outlined in white. RN legend and fuselage serial in white; 'Royal Navy' in black underwing in place of serials. '6' on nose-wheel door in black; note no inboard cannon.

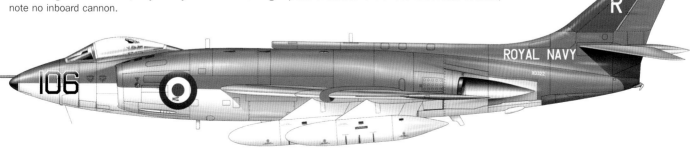

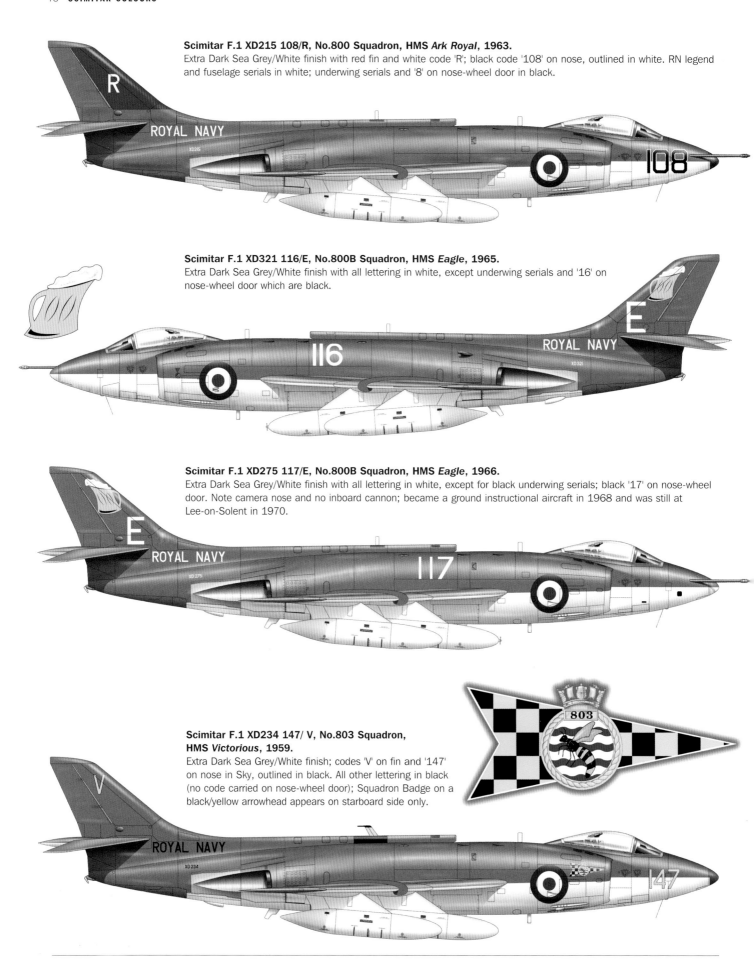

Scimitar F.1 XD215 108/R, No.800 Squadron, HMS *Ark Royal*, 1963.
Extra Dark Sea Grey/White finish with red fin and white code 'R'; black code '108' on nose, outlined in white. RN legend and fuselage serials in white; underwing serials and '8' on nose-wheel door in black.

Scimitar F.1 XD321 116/E, No.800B Squadron, HMS *Eagle*, 1965.
Extra Dark Sea Grey/White finish with all lettering in white, except underwing serials and '16' on nose-wheel door which are black.

Scimitar F.1 XD275 117/E, No.800B Squadron, HMS *Eagle*, 1966.
Extra Dark Sea Grey/White finish with all lettering in white, except for black underwing serials; black '17' on nose-wheel door. Note camera nose and no inboard cannon; became a ground instructional aircraft in 1968 and was still at Lee-on-Solent in 1970.

Scimitar F.1 XD234 147/ V, No.803 Squadron, HMS *Victorious*, 1959.
Extra Dark Sea Grey/White finish; codes 'V' on fin and '147' on nose in Sky, outlined in black. All other lettering in black (no code carried on nose-wheel door); Squadron Badge on a black/yellow arrowhead appears on starboard side only.

Scimitar F.1 XD264 154/V, No.803 Squadron, HMS *Victorious*, 1959.
Extra Dark Sea Grey/White finish; codes 'V' on fin and '154' on nose in Sky,
outlined in black. All other lettering in black (no code carried on nose-wheel
door); Squadron Badge appears on starboard side only.

Scimitar F.1 XD214 146/H, No.803 Naval Air Squadron, HMS *Hermes*, 1962.
Extra Dark Sea Grey/White finish with all lettering in white, except for underwing serial and '146' on nose-wheel door;
no inboard cannon. Note camera nose fitted; Squadron Badge on starboard side only (see XD215 156/H).

Scimitar F.1 XD225 154/H, No.803 Squadron, HMS *Hermes*, 1964.
Extra Dark Sea Grey/White finish with all lettering in white, except underwing serials and '154' on nose-wheel door which
are in black; yellow/black checks on fin. No inboard cannon.

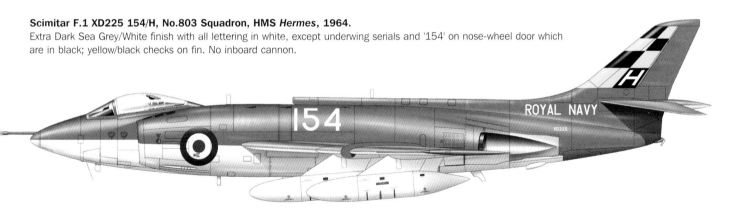

Scimitar F.1 XD250 147/H, No.803 Squadron, HMS *Hermes*, 1963.
Extra Dark Sea Grey/White finish with all lettering in white, except underwing serials and '147'
on nose-wheel door which are in black; yellow/black chequer on fin. No inboard cannon.

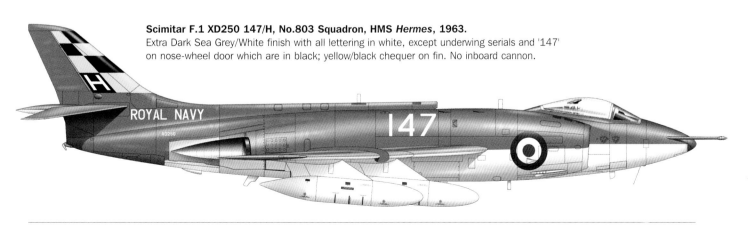

Scimitar F.1 XD235 149/R, No.803 Squadron, HMS *Ark Royal*, 1965.
Extra Dark Sea Grey/White finish with all lettering in white, except underwing serials and '149' on nose-wheel door which were in black; yellow/black chequer on fin. No inboard cannon.

Scimitar F.1 XD324 033/R, No.803 Squadron, HMS *Ark Royal*, 1966.
Extra Dark Sea Grey/White finish with all lettering in white, except underwing serials and '33' on nose-wheel door; yellow/black chequer on fin. No inboard cannon; became ground instructional airframe in 1968 and was at Lee-on-Solent in 1970.

Scimitar F.1 XD325 165/H, No.804 Squadron, HMS *Hermes*, 1960.
Extra Dark Sea Grey/White finish with lettering in black, except RN legend on fuselage which is in white; '165' on nose outlined in white. White fin with unit's 'tiger's head' Motif in black and yellow; '5' in black on nose-wheel door.

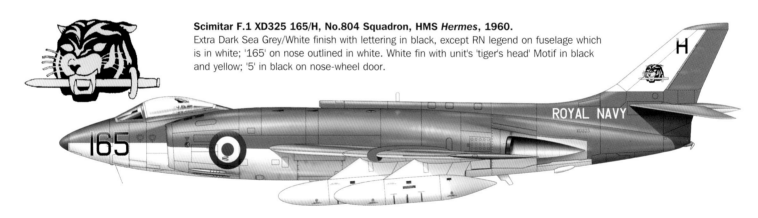

Scimitar F.1 XD323 162/H, No.804 Squadron, HMS *Hermes*, 1960-61.
Extra Dark Sea Grey/White finish with all lettering in black, except RN legend on fuselage which is white; '162' on nose outlined in white. White fin with unit's 'tiger's head' Motif in yellow and black; '2' in black on nose-wheel door. Note red front tip to underwing tanks.

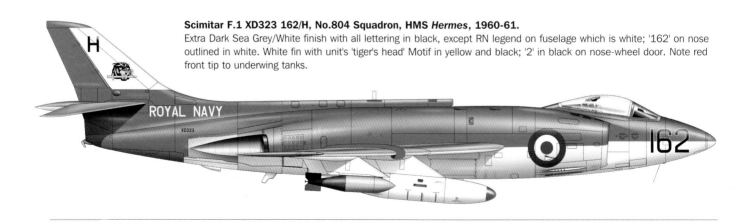

Scimitar F.1 XD248 195/R, No.807 Squadron, HMS *Ark Royal*, summer 1959.
Extra Dark Sea Grey/White finish with RN legend and serials in black; code 'R' on fin in white. Nose code '195' in light blue, outlined in black; '5' in black on nose-wheel door.

Scimitar F.1 XD268 194/R, No.807 Squadron, Hal-Far, Malta, early 1960.
Extra Dark Sea Grey/White finish with serials and RN legend in black; code 'R' on fin in white. Nose code '194' in light blue, outlined in black; '4' in black on nose-wheel door.

Scimitar F.1 XD319 192/R, No.807 Squadron, HMS *Ark Royal*, 1960.
Extra Dark Sea Grey/White finish with RN legend and serials in black; nose code in black, outlined in white. Code 'R' on fin in white; '2' repeated in black on nose-wheel door which was also outlined in black.

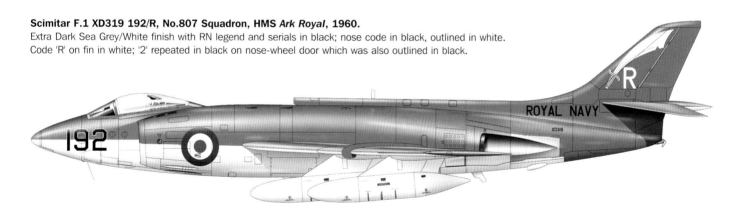

Scimitar F.1 XD319 192/C, No.807 Squadron, HMS *Centaur*, 1961.
Extra Dark Sea Grey/White finish with all lettering in white, except underwing serials; nose code in black, outlined in white. 'C' on fin in white; '2' on nose-wheel door which is outlined in black.

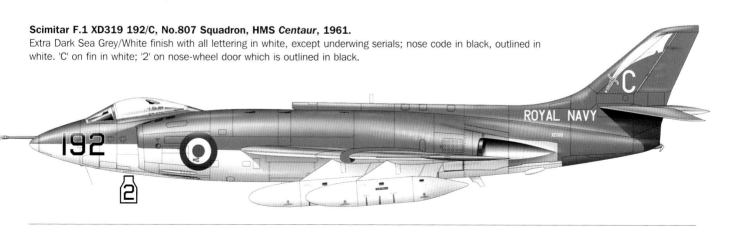

Scimitar F.1 XD224 615/LM, No.736 Squadron, Lossiemouth, 1960.
Extra Dark Sea Grey/White finish with lettering in black, except for code 'LM' on fin which is in white; nose code '615' is white on a blue rectangle. Squadron Badge carried on starboard side only; '15' in black on nose-wheel door.

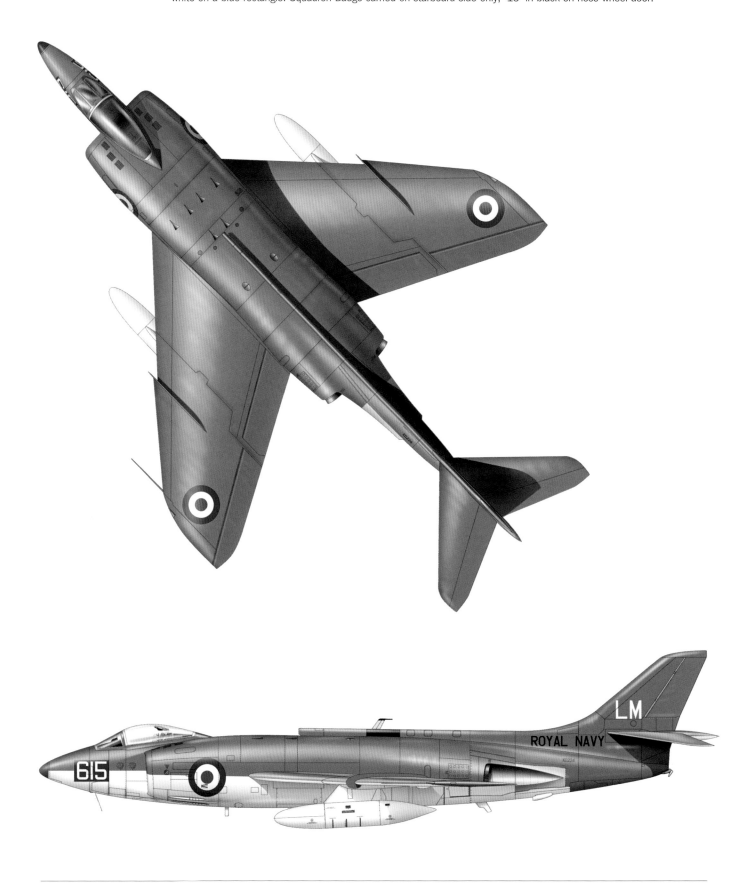

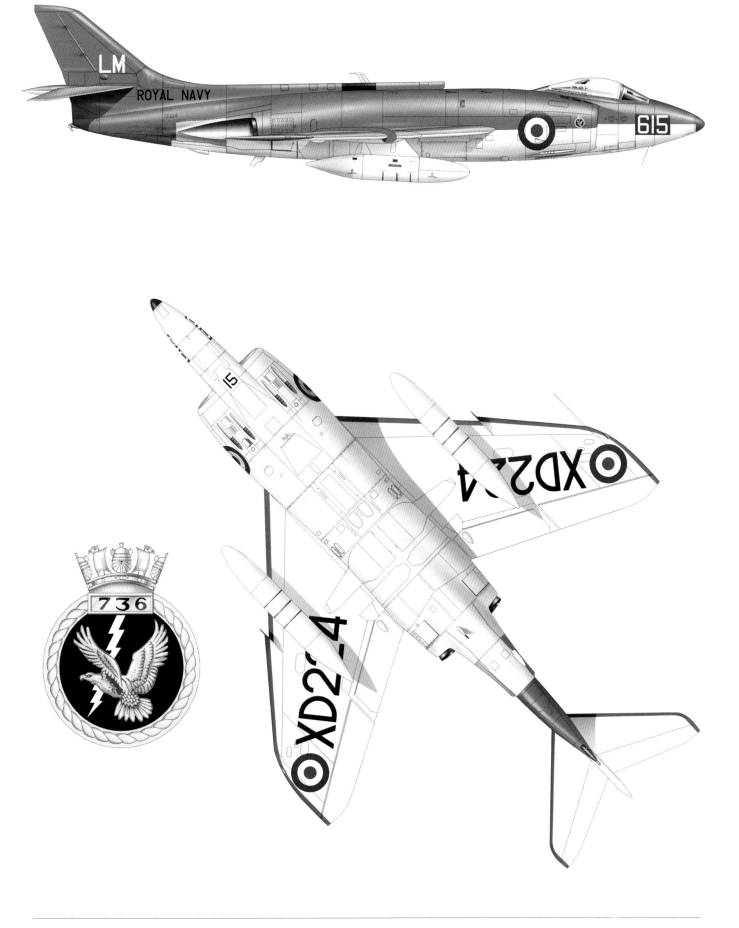

Scimitar F.1 XD229, Royal Aircraft Establishment.
Light blue overall with white tail surfaces; black leading edges of fin and tailplane. Lettering in black.

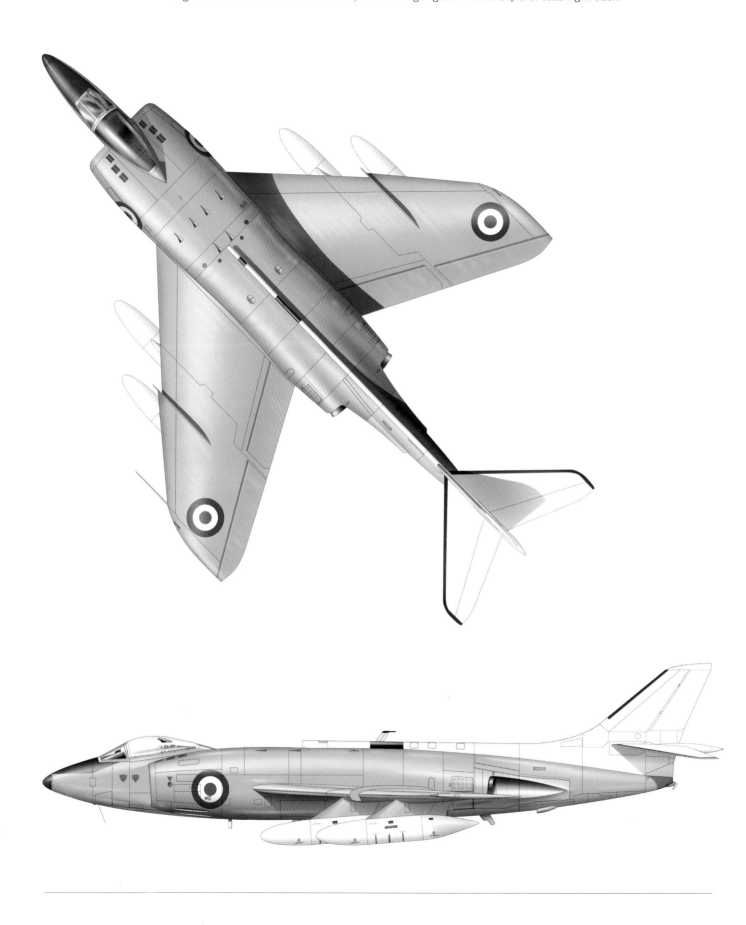

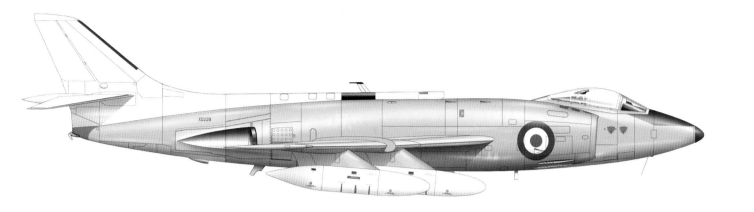

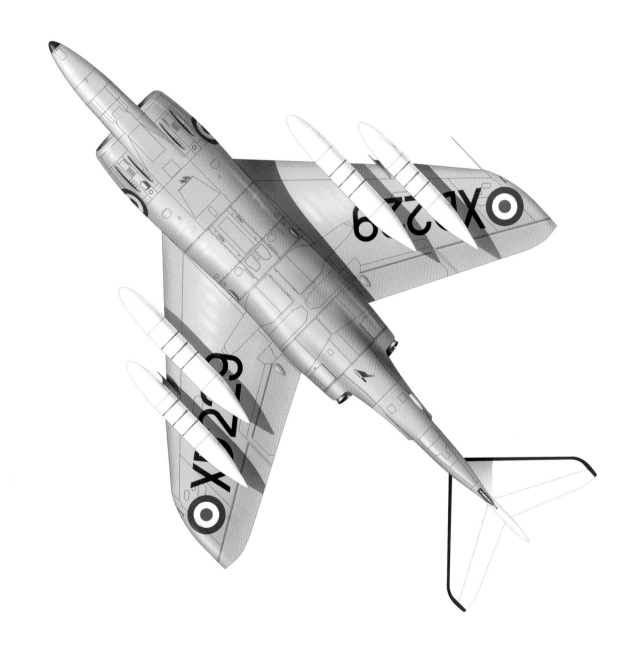

Scimitar F.1 XD265 105/R, No.800 Squadron, HMS *Ark Royal*, 1961.
All lettering in white, except nose code '105' which is in black, outlined in white, and underwing lettering in black.
Red fin with white code. '5' repeated on nose-wheel door

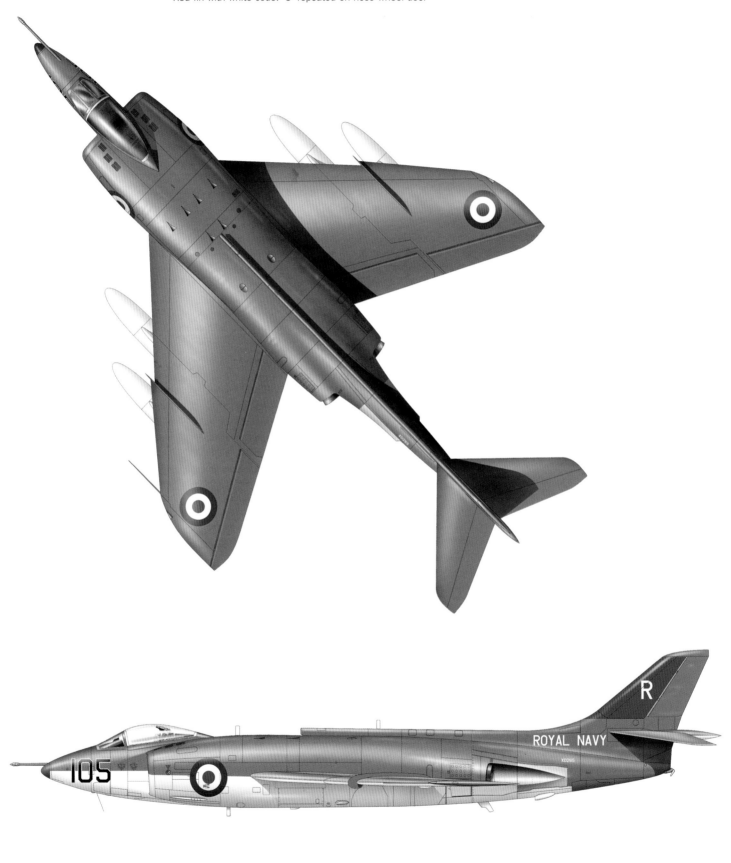

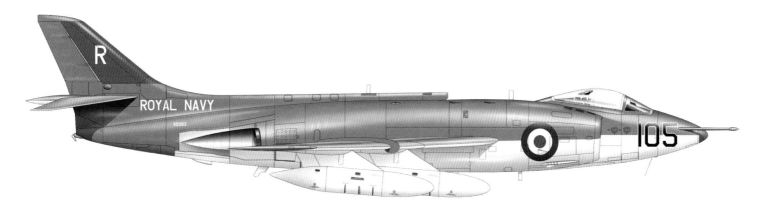

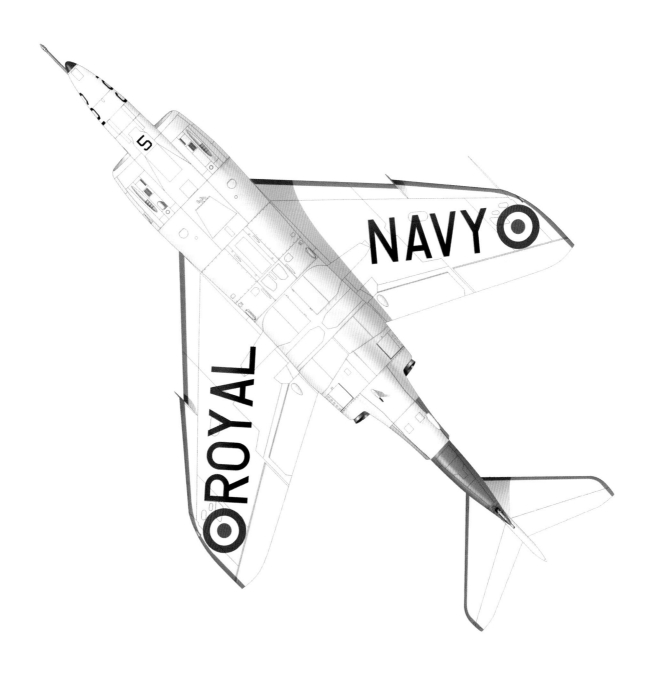

Chapter 7: **ALL AT SEA**

Above: *HMS Ark Royal hosts a visiting US Navy Douglas A-4 Skyhawk which is seen in company with Scimitar 109/R belonging to No.800 Squadron. The twin 20mm cannon protruding from the leading edge of the A-4's wing look quite imposing, but they provided nothing like the firepower of the Scimitar's four 30mm cannon which, prior to the age of the air-to-air missile, offered devastating firepower. FAA Museum*

Opposite top: *192/R, No.807 Squadron aboard HMS Ark Royal being prepared for an exercise in September 1960. Note the pilots name in white on the engine air intake. FAA Museum*

Below: *Close up detail of a Bullpup installation. Note that the Scimitar has been raised on jacks.* Fleet Air Arm Museum

Below: *This photograph was captioned as '…Lieutenant Mills departs'. Having said that of course, 166/H of No.804 Squadron seen aboard HMS* Hermes *in 1960, doesn't appear quiet ready for an immediate departure…!* FAA Museum

Right: *103/R of No.800 Squadron.* FAA Museum

Below: *F.1 XD280 104/R, No.800 Squadron, HMS Ark Royal, 28th April 1960, off Cyprus. This aircraft, flown by Lt P Banfield, had suffered a hydraulics failure and as a consequence, although the nose-wheel, flaps and hook operated normally, the main undercarriage didn't and the pilot had no option but to fly into the barrier. Following the accident a small fire ensued but this was quickly extinguished; XD280 was later repaired ashore.* FAA Museum

Above and below: *F.1 XD325 024/R, No.803 Squadron, HMS* Ark Royal, *7th March 1966, Indian Ocean. Flown by Lt T Notley, this aircraft was unable to lower its nose-wheel and, with no diversion options available, the pilot had to land back aboard and engage the barrier. The resulting* damage was extensive and XD325's nose-wheel was forced through the foreword fuselage which was torn open. Fortunately the pilot was uninjured, whilst the aircraft was beyond repair and ultimately reduced to spares. Brian Lowe

Right: *A No.803 Squadron Scimitar lands aboard HMS* Victorious. *A Sea Venom can be seen in the foreground and three escorting destroyers off the port rear quarter.* FAA Museum

Below right: *Less dramatic and less damaging was this incident aboard HMS* Victorious *in 1959 when the vessel experienced severe weather and heeled to one side. The tractor towing Scimitar 147/V at that moment, was unable to prevent the aircraft slipping towards and then over the deck edge, with the results shown.* FAA Museum

Opposite top: *The original photograph is captioned as '...a pre launch deck scene on a really dirty day aboard HMS* Victorious'. *It ought to be pointed out however that the particularly dark 'weather' above the Sea Venoms is created by their engine starting cartridges.* FAA Museum

Opposite bottom: *HMS* Victorious *negotiating the Suez canal on either the 2nd or 4th December 1961.* FAA Museum

Above: *HMS* Ark Royal *with a No.800 Squadron Scimitar on deck accompanied by a Westland Wessex helicopter. The vessel beyond is HMS* Devonshire, *a guided missile destroyer and the first of an entirely new breed of vessel to enter service with the Royal Navy in which, for the first time, guided missiles formed an extensive element of the ship's weapon systems. Eight vessels of this class were built, several of which* later received a quad Exocet surface-to-surface missile installation in lieu of 'B' their 4.5in turret. FAA Museum

Below: *Panels off. 103/R of No. 800 Squadron aboard HMS* Ark Royal. FAA Museum

Above: *F.1 XD324 033/R, No.803 Squadron, HMS* Ark Royal. *Catapult bridles can be seen placed on the deck in readiness.* Brian Lowe

Below: *A Scimitar of No.807 Squadron, possibly XD236 195/C (HMS Centaur) with two Sea Vixens aboard HMS* Centaur *during October 1961. The Sea Vixens were conducting Firestreak air-to-air missile trials at this time.* FAA Museum

Above: *Cold weather trials aboard HMS* Ark Royal *(RO9) in February 1961. As 190/R of No.807 Squadron is prepared for launching, an aircraft handler is apparently pulling a launching bridle from a rack positioned just below the deck edge!* FAA Museum

Below: *HMS* Hermes *(R12). Nominally a member of the four-strong Centaur class of aircraft carriers, Hermes was laid down in 1944 but not finally completed until 1959. During the intervening period enormous strides had been taken with the development of naval aircraft and methods of their operation at sea and Hermes, when completed, incorporated these changes. However by 1970 Hermes was removed from service as a fixed wing carrier and was converted to become a commando and helicopter carrier, it having become apparent during the 1960s that the vessel was a little too short to operate Scimitars and Sea Vixens safely. Hermes served with distinction during the Falklands War operating Sea Harriers and Harriers from its deck, after which the vessel was sold to India in 1987 as INS* Viraat. FAA Museum

Above: HMS Ark Royal, *was a sister ship of HMS* Eagle *(R05). They were the largest and possibly the most effective aircraft carriers ever operated by the Royal Navy. Both underwent extensive overhauls and rebuilding throughout their respective lives and were able to operate reasonably large complements of aircraft, which, inevitably, reduced in number as naval aircraft grew ever larger and heavier.*

Below: HMS Eagle *was, controversially, taken out of service in 1972 and held as a source of spares for* Ark Royal *which had been modernised to* operate Phantoms. *In December 1978,* Ark Royal, *even more controversially, despite being in a mechanically poor condition was also taken out of service, leaving the Royal Navy devoid of a conventional aircraft carrier, a capability sorely missed during the Falklands War in 1982. It is perhaps worth speculating as to whether that conflict would have occurred if the RN had still possessed a conventional aircraft carrier force! (as opposed to a 'Harrier carrier').* Eagle *was broken-up from October 1978 and* Ark Royal *from 1980. Both FAA Museum*

Above: *HMS* Centaur *(R06). The nameship of a class of four aircraft carriers,* Centaur *was the only one of the four to operate as a fixed-wing carrier throughout its operational career, (the others being* Albion, Bulwark *and* Hermes*).* Centaur *never benefited from the extensive modifications that* Hermes, *a near-sister received and consequently* Centaur *was somewhat shorter and narrower than* Hermes *with the result that the operation of powerful, large and heavy aircraft such as the Scimitar and Sea Vixen was even more marginal than was the case for*

Hermes. *Even so, despite its limitations the vessel served its purpose remaining in service until paid off in late 1965, thereafter becoming an accommodation ship until sold for scrap in 1972. The size of the aircraft seen on deck in this photograph indicates how small* Centaur *was, even so the true sense of scale is hard to appreciate, but for comparison* Centaur *displaced approximately 27,000 tons at deep load, whereas* Eagle, *displaced 50,000 tons at deep load. Brian Lowe*

Left: *HMS* Victorious *(R38) entering Naples Bay, dwarfed by the 78,000 ton USS* Saratoga *(CVA-60) in the background.* FAA Museum

Opposite top: *HMS* Victorious *berthed at Gibraltar in October 1960.* FAA Museum

Opposite bottom: *HMS* Hermes *with a crowded flight deck.* FAA Museum

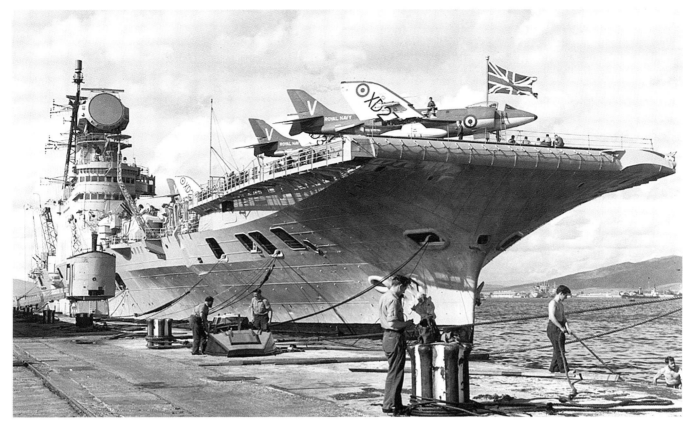

Appendix I: **SCIMITAR IN DETAIL**

A range of detail photographs of XD317.
Peter Jefferies

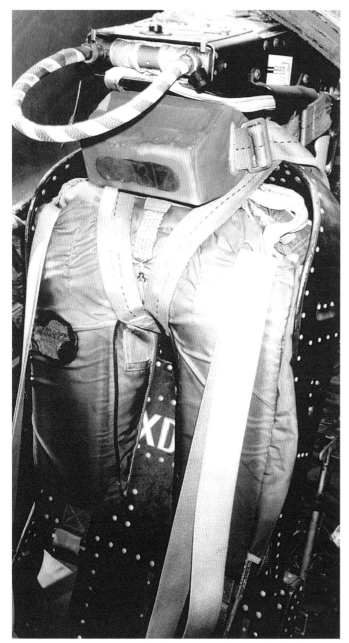

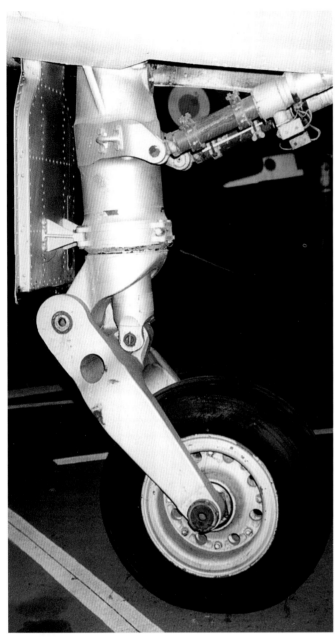

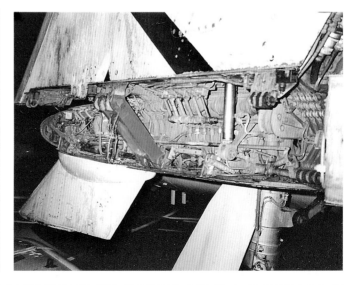

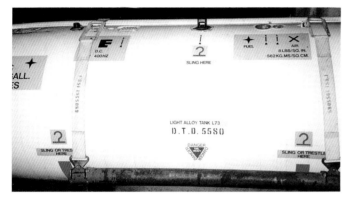

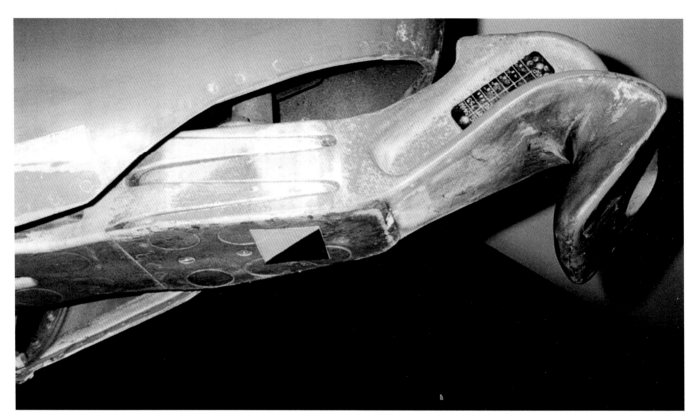

The Scimitar leaves the fleet.

From FOAC (Flag)

To   The Commanding Officer
      803 Squadron
Info. ARK ROYAL

Precedence   Routine

Classification U/C

D.T.G.   011054²

Special Instructions

1.   In saying goodbye to a fine and spirited squadron I am conscious that this is a sad occasion. The SCIMITAR is leaving the Fleet and the squadron disbanding.

2.   803 is to be congratulated on the manner in which it has met and tackled some particularly testing situations. I have been particularly impressed to see in these last months how well you have managed to get these old aircraft working probably better than ever before.

3.   Good luck to you all. I shall personally miss the black and yellow chequers very much.

D.T.G.   011054² - OCT - 66

Orig/R.O.   SAVO/RA

Action   CO 803

Ref.

Dst.   C.R.02

Transit Instructions ✓14   TOA INTERWAR 1-OCT-66

Appendix II: **TECHNICAL DATA**

PROTOTYPES

Type 505

Span:	35ft. Folded approx 25ft
Length:	46ft 8in
Height:	To top of folded wing panel only 9ft
Engine:	Two Rolls-Royce Axial Flow AJ.65 turbojets
Fuel Capacity:	405 Imperial gallons
Weight:	Basic 12,220lb
	Max 15,500lb
Max speed:	680mph @ sea level, 630mph @ 20,000ft, 590mph @ 45,000ft
Climb to:	25,000ft: 1 min. 12 secs
Climb to:	45,000ft: 3 mins.
Ceiling:	Not known
Range (nm):	Not known
Armament:	Initially 4.5in RCL recoil-less gun, but later amended to use the MK213/30 (later ADEN) 30mm cannon
Production:	Mock-up only

Type 508 (to N.9/47)

First Flight:	31st August 1951
Span:	40ft. Folded approx 26ft
Length:	46ft 8in
Height:	To top of fin 13ft
Engine:	Two Rolls-Royce AJ.65 axial turbojets
Fuel Capacity:	415 Imperial gallons
Weight:	Basic 14,140lb
	Max 17,500lb
Max speed	660mph @ sea level, 625mph @ 25,000ft, 575mph @ 45,000ft
Initial rate of climb:	18,500ft/min @ sea level
Climb to	25,000ft: 1 min 45 secs
Climb to	45,000ft: 4 mins 30 secs
Ceiling:	45,000ft
Range (nm):	Not known
Armament:	Four MK213/30 30mm cannon (later developed into the ADEN cannon) - never actually fitted
Production:	3 Ordered, only 1 built as true Type 508 (VX133)

Type 529 (to N.9/47)

First Flight:	29th August 1952
Span:	40ft, folded approx 26ft
Length:	46ft 8in
Height:	To top of fin 13ft
Engine:	Two Rolls-Royce AJ.65 axial turbojets
Fuel Capacity:	415 Imperial gallons
Weight:	Basic 14,140lb
	Max 17,500lb
Max speed:	660mph @ sea level, 625mph @ 25,000ft 575mph @ 45,000ft
Initial rate of climb:	18,500ft/min @ sea level
Climb to:	25,000ft: 1 min 45 secs
Climb to:	45,000ft: 4 mins. 30 secs
Ceiling:	45,000ft
Range (nm):	Not known
Armament:	Four ADEN 30mm cannon
Production:	1 (VX136) - originally ordered as Type 508, but modified and allocated a new type number

Type 525 (to N.9/47)

First Flight:	27th April 1954
Span:	37ft 2in, folded 20ft
Length:	53ft, fuselage only 49ft 1in
Height:	To top of fin 15ft 1in, to top of wings folded 15ft 7in
Engine:	Two Rolls-Royce AJ.65 axial turbojets
Fuel Capacity:	630 Imperial gallons plus 430 Imperial gallons in drop tanks
Weight:	Max 28,169 lb
Max speed	660mph @ sea level, 625mph @ 25,000ft, 575mph @ 45,000ft
Initial rate of climb:	18,500ft/min @ sea level
Ceiling:	45,000ft
Range (nm):	Not known
Armament:	Four ADEN 30mm cannon
Production:	1 built (VX138), although originally ordered as Type 508

Type 544 (N.113D)

First Flight:	20th January 1956
Span:	37ft 2in, folded 20ft 6½in
Length:	50ft
Height:	To top of fin 17ft
Engine:	Two Rolls-Royce AJ.65 axial turbojets
Fuel Capacity:	415 Imperial gallons
Weight:	Max 24,000 lb
Max speed:	710mph @ sea level with reheat, 602mph without reheat, 636mph @ 45,000ft with reheat
Rate of climb:	18,000ft/min @ sea level, 2,000ft/min @ 45,000ft
Ceiling:	49,000ft
Range (nm):	Not known
Armament:	Four 30mm ADEN cannon plus option to install Blue Sky or Blue Jay missiles and capacity to carry rockets and drop tanks on the four wing strong points
Production:	3 (WT854, WT859 & WW134)

SCIMITAR F.1

First Flight:	11th January 1957 (XD212)
Span:	37ft 2in, To wing hinge point 20ft 6½in *
Length:	To tip of radome 55ft 3¼in, to tip of refuelling probe 57ft 7in *
Height:	17ft 4in, to top of folded outer wing panel only 16ft 0in *
Undercarriage track:	14ft 1in *
Engine:	Two Rolls-Royce RA24 or RA28 Avon engines producing 10,000lb thrust each. Later these were replaced with 200 series Avons
Weight:	Basic 23,962lb, Max 34,200lb
Max speed:	727mph @ sea level, 516mph @ 30,000ft
Rate of climb:	6 mins 38 secs to 45,000ft
Ceiling:	46,000ft
Range (nm):	1,422 miles @ 35,000ft
Armament:	Four 30mm ADEN cannon and four 1,000lb freefall bombs or four Bullpup air-to-ground missiles or four Sidewinder air-to-air missiles. Alternatively four 200 Imperial gallon drop tanks.
Production:	100 ordered but only 76 actually built

* All dimensions relate to the airframe on jacks, with oleos extended, wheels just touching the ground and tailplane in the fully drooped position.

Opposite: *Four No.807 Squadron Scimitars perform formation aerobatics in 1950.* via Tony Buttler

Appendix III: **SCIMITAR SQUADRONS**

No.700 Squadron

Began to operate Scimitar: 12th March 1958
UK bases: Ford 3/58-9/58, Yeovilton 9/58-2/59
Re-equipped: February 1959 (last Scimitar relinquished)
Variants operated: Scimitar F Mk 1

No.700X Squadron

Began to operate Scimitar: 27th August 1957
UK base: Ford 8/57-5/58
Disbanded: 29th May 1958
Variants operated: Scimitar F Mk 1

No.736 Squadron

Began to operate Scimitar: June 1959
UK base: Lossiemouth 6/59-3/65
Disbanded: 26th March 1965 (remnants formed
    No.764B Squadron)
Re-equipped: Buccaneer S.1 from 3/65
Variants operated: Scimitar F Mk 1

No.764 Squadron

Began to operate Scimitar: February 1959 until
    May 1959 only
UK base: Lossiemouth, for full details see main text

No.764B Squadron

Began to operate Scimitar: March 1965
UK base: Lossiemouth 3/65-11/65
Disbanded: 23rd November 1965
Variants operated: Scimitar F Mk 1

No.800 Squadron

Began to operate Scimitar: July 1959
UK base: Lossiemouth 7/59-2/64
On board: HMS *Ark Royal* 3/60-9/60, 10/60-11/60,
11/61-12/61, 3/62-6/62, 2/3/63, 5/63 & 7/63
Foreign detachments: Hal Far, Malta 11/60, 12/61-
1/62. Tengah, Singapore 6/62-7/62, 9/62, 7/63 & 8/63.
Embakasi 6/63 & 10/63-11/63
Disbanded: 25th February 1964
Reformed: 18/3/64 with Buccaneer S.1
Variants operated: Scimitar F Mk 1

No.800B Squadron

Began to operate Scimitar: 9th September 1964
UK bases: Lossiemouth 9/64-12/64 & 5/65-8/65.
Yeovilton 8/66
On board: HMS *Eagle* 12/64-5/65 & 8/65-11/65
Foreign detachments: Changi, Singapore 11-65-7/66
Disbanded: 14th August 1966
Variants Operated: Scimitar F Mk 1

No.803 Squadron

Began to operate Scimitar: 3rd June 1958
UK bases: Lossiemouth 6/58-9/58, 1/59-2/59, 3/59-
5/59, 8/59-9/59, 9/59-10/59, 12/59, 2/60. 12/61-2/62,
3/62-5/62, 10/62-11/62, 10/63-11/63, 12/63-1/64,
7/64-8/64, 9/64-11/64, 12/64-1/65, 3/65-6/65, 6/66-
8/66 & 10/66. Yeovilton 5/59, 9/59-10/59, 12/59-2/59,
2/60-8/60, 12/61, 10/62 (transit), 9/63 (detachment),
6/64-7/64, 8/64-9/64, 11/64 (detachment)
On board: HMS *Victorious* 9/58-10/58, 12/58-1/59,
2/59-3/59, 5/59-8/59, 9/59, 10/59-12/59, 2/60, 10/60-
11/60, 11/60-12/60, 1/61-3/61, 4/61-5/61, 6/61-9/61,
10/61-12/61 & 2/62-3/62. HMS *Hermes* 8/60-10/60,
5/62-6/62, 11/62-12/62 & 11/63-12/63. HMS *Ark Royal*
12/64, 1/65-3/65, 6/65-7/65, 12/65-1/66, 1/66-3/66,
3/66-6/66 & 8/66-10/66
Foreign detachments: Hal Far, Malta 10/58, 11/58-
12/58, 11/60, 6/62 & 9/62-10/62. Hyéres 10/58-11/58.
Tengah, Singapore 3/61-4/61, 9/61-10/61, 12/62-1/63 &
3/63-4/63. Butterworth, Malaya 5/61-6/61 & 11/65.
North Front 7/62-8/62. Changi, Singapore 7/65-8/65,
10/65-11/65, 11/65, 1/66 & 3/66
Reformed: 3/7/67 with Buccaneer S.1
Disbanded: 1st October 1966
Variants Operated: Scimitar F Mk 1

No.804 Squadron

Started to operate Scimitar: 1st March 1960
UK base: Lossiemouth 3/60-7/60, 10/60-11/60,
4/61-5/61 & 9/61
On board: HMS *Hermes* 7/60-10/60, 11/60-12/60,
1/61-4/61 & 5/61-9/61
Foreign detachments: North Front 11/60.
Tengah, Singapore 12/60-1/61
Disbanded: 15th September 1961
Variants operated: Scimitar F Mk 1

No.807 Squadron

Began to operate Scimitar: 1st October 1958
UK bases: Lossiemouth 10/58-6/59, 7/59-9/59, 9/59-
1/60, 9/60-10/60, 2/61-4/61, 9/61-10/61 & 4/62-5/62.
Yeovilton 6/59 (detachment). West Freugh 7/59
(detachment). Culdrose 7/59 (detachment)
On board: HMS *Victorious* 1/60. HMS *Ark Royal* 2/60-
3/60, 10/60-11/60, 11/60-12/60 & 12/60-2/61.
HMS *Centaur* 4/61, 5/61-6/61, 6/61-7/61, 10/61-11/61,
11/61-4/62 & 4/62-5/62
Foreign Detachments: Hal Far, Malta 4/60-6/60, 7/60-
8/60, 11/60, 12/60, 4/61-5/61, 8/61-9/61, 11/61 &
4/62. North Front 6/60-7/60 & 6/61. Khormaksar, Aden
7/61-8/61
Disbanded: 15th May 1962
Variants operated: Scimitar F Mk 1

OTHER UNITS WHICH HAVE USED THE SCIMITAR

Royal Navy - Other
RNAY Fleetlands, Gosport, Hampshire
February 1958 - 21st March 1968.
Operated as the RN Aircraft Repair Yard for the Scimitar throughout its career.

RNAS Brawdy
Maintenance Test Pilots School
All test pilots operated at the Aircraft Handling Units were trained here, including those that were to fly the Scimitar from RNAY Fleetlands. The unit undertook this role in relation to the Scimitar from 1958 through to 1968.

AHU (Aircraft Handling Unit) Lossiemouth
March 1958-1961
This unit received newly built Scimitars from the manufacturer and carried out the acceptance checks before passing them on to the units.

CIVIL ORGANISATIONS

Shorts Ferry Flight
This company was contracted to the Admiralty to supply ferry pilots and it operated with the Scimitar in this role from 12/60 through to 6/66, when the contract expired.

Airwork Limited, Fleet Requirements Unit
The unit operated the Scimitar in the Fleet Requirements role from June 1966, although it had a Scimitar (XD267) from November 1965 for familiarisation. The type remained in use until late 1969, or early 1970. The last ever Scimitar flight was made from RNAS Brawdy (where the Airwork FRU operated) to Southend Airport on the 12th February 1971 with XD244.

GOVERNMENT AGENCIES

A&AEE Boscombe Down
This test facility included C Squadron, the Naval test unit, and it operated various Scimitars right from early trials with the Type 508 until the final acceptance trials during 1961, although others may have been used after this date for specific 'one-off' trials.

Royal Aircraft Establishment
Various tests and trials using the Scimitar were undertaken by the RAE both from Farnborough and Bedford. Some of the weapons testing was done over the West Freugh ranges by Scimitars flown from Farnborough, while Bedford was the location of many of the deck handling and arrester trials for the type.

Proof & Experimental Establishment
Based in a bleak corner of Foulness Island, Shoeburyness is where most ballistic testing is carried out and it is was here in early 1970 that retired Scimitars started to arrive. Initially five obsolete airframes arrived, having flown into nearby Southend Airport before being moved by road to P&EE. These were followed in late 1970 with the arrival of the ex-FRU machines from Hurn (XD234, 241, 244, 322

& 333). These airframes remained on site, with a few moves back and forth from No.71 MU (Abingdon) and the ranges at Aberporth & Pendine, until the late 1980s, by which time only a few remained. In 1990 these were put up for sale by the MoD and purchased by scrap merchants Mayer & Perry, who removed the airframes during April 1991. Although the bulk of the airframes were in very poor condition a number of cockpit sections were saved and sold to various collections via Parkhouse Aviation.

Period advertisement for the Supermarine Scimitar from Vickers-Armstrong (Aircraft) Limited. via Author

Appendix IV: **SCIMITAR PRODUCTION**

Serial numbers in **bold** text indicate the aircraft is extant at the time of going to press.

Specification Number: N.9/47
 Contract Number: 6/Acft/1508/CB.7b dtd 13/11/47
 Type 508 Prototype
 Quantity: 3
VX133 VA, Hursley Park by road to A&AEE; FF 31/08/51 then to VA, Chilbolton; To SBAC Farnborough for display 11/09/51, Returned VA, Chilbolton 17/09/51; To A&AEE for trials 11/51, damaged Cat.3 5/12/51; To VA, Chilbolton 12/51 to 09/04/52 then to RAE Bedford for arrester trials 29/04/52; Returned VA, Chilbolton 2/05/52; To RAE Farnborough then Returned to VA, Chilbolton *en-route* via Ford for deck trials 17/05/52; HMS *Eagle* for arresting trials 28/05/52 Returned to VA, Chilbolton 29/05/052; Took part in Lee-on-Solent 'At Home' day but damaged in flight 12/07/52; To RAE Farnborough for measurement of loads during arrested landing 13/07/53; To RAE Bedford 22/08/55; On HMS *Bulwark* for trials 31/10/55; To RAE Bedford 14/11/55; To HM Dockyard Devonport for trials on HMS *Centaur* for hangar desk strength tests 24/09/56; RAE Bedford 28/11/56 and loan made permanent 18/09/59; Released from trials by NAD/RAE Bedford 29/03/63: Noted at MARSTU Lee-on-Solent 26/11/63, still there 25/12/63; To SAH Culdrose, became GI Class II Instructional Airframe A2529 7/01/64; To Predannack for fire fighting training 1/08/70 and totally consumed by 1984.
VX136 Completed as Type 529, FF VA, Chilbolton 29/09/52; To SBAC Farnborough 31/08/52, Returned VA, Chilbolton 8/09/52; To RAE Farnborough for tail-down landing trials 20/04/53, force landing 5/05/53; Returned to VA, Chilbolton for survey and repair 8/05/53; Returned to RAE Farnborough for acceleration trials 22/06/53; Returned to VA, Chilbolton to resume development trials 10/07/53; Start work-up for deck trials at RAE Farnborough 1/10/53, HMS *Eagle* for deck trials 3-4/11/53; Returned RAE Farnborough 18/11/53; To VA, Chilbolton 19/11/53 to resume development trials; Partial wheels-up landing at VA, Chilbolton, not repairable on site, 2/12/53; Put into temporary storage at VA, Chilbolton 13/01/54; Authority granted to SOC 27/10/54; Fuselage & wings for ballistic targets to P&EE Shoeburyness 30/07/56, engine to RAE Bedford; Nose and cockpit sections to RAE Farnborough 12/58; Remainder scrapped at Shoeburyness 09/61.
VX138 Built as Type 525; To A&AEE Boscombe Down by road 25/04/54; FF A&AEE Boscombe Down 27/04/54. Returned VA, Chilbolton 6/05/54; To SBAC Farnborough for display 7-12/09/54, Returned VA, Chilbolton 13/09/54; By road to Hursley Park Experimental Dept for fitment of flap blowing system in early 1955; Returned by road to VA, Chilbolton; To A&AEE Boscombe Down for trials 4/07/55; Aircraft spun in from 3,000ft 2 miles SSE of airfield Cat 5 5/07/55; Wreckage moved to VA, Chilbolton and SOC 30/01/56.

Specification Number: N.113D
 Contract Number: 6/Acft/6579/CB.7(b) dtd 29/03/51
 Type 544 Prototype
 Quantity: 2
WT854 By road to A&AEE Boscombe Down 14/01/56; FF A&AEE Boscombe Down 19/01/56; To VA, Chilbolton 30/01/56; To VA, Wisley 25/02/56; To RAE Bedford 6/03/56; Returned to VA, Chilbolton 10/03/56; To A&AEE Boscombe Down 22/03/56; HMS *Ark Royal* for deck landing trials 5/04/56; Damaged wheels due to take-off with brake on, Returned to *Ark Royal* safely for wheel change 09/04/56; To VA, Chilbolton 12/04/56; To VA, Wisley for mods to wings and tailplanes 16/04/56; Received slight damage in landing with nose-wheel retracted 20/08/56; To SBAC Farnborough for display 4-7/09/56; To A&AEE Boscombe Down for trials of modifications 17/10/56; Returned to VA, Wisley(?) 27/10/56; Modified nose for flight-refuelling (dummy) trials 26/11/56; At VA, Wisley for trials with Valiant tanker 1/01/57; Nose sent to VA, Wisley for modification after unsuccessful flight-refuelling trials 5/02/57; Returned to Eastleigh for completion of trials 12/02/57; Undertook measured take-off 11/03/57; Arrested Dummy Deck Landings undertaken 21/03/57, 24/03/57, 2/04/57 & 4/04/57; Embarked on HMS *Ark Royal* 5/04/57; Autostabiliser tests 11/04/57; Aileron configuration tests satisfactory 24/04/57; At A&AEE Boscombe Down but still on firm's charge 26/04/57; Undertook trials (speed with flight refuelling probe) 24/04/57, fuel jettison instrumentation - deferred) 15/05/57 and (550Knots IAS

behind other Scimitar) 16/05/57; Jet exhaust fairings being fitted 6/06/57; To A&AEE Boscombe Down 23/08/57; To VA, Wisley 17/09/57, engine inhibited and disposal instructions awaited 21/05/58; Allocated to RAE Bedford for various trials, including those to potential destruction 16/12/59; Allocated to Class II GI at AES Arbroath 25/10/60, but cancelled; Released by NAD/RAE Bedford 6/11/64 and moved by road to SAH Culdrose; To P&EE Shoeburyness 1967 and subsequently destroyed in ballistic firing trials.
WT859 To A&AEE Boscombe Down by road and flown 26/06/56, Returned to VA, Wisley 06/56-08/56 (date unknown), Returned to A&AEE Boscombe Down 28/08/56; To VA, Wisley 30/08/56 and converted to flap blowing system 8/10/56; Modifications continued at Hurlsey Park 10/12/56; By road to A&AEE Boscombe Down 27/12/56; Damaged Cat HC 17/06/57 and Cat LC 13/07/57; C(A) release issued A&AEE Boscombe Down 21/03/58; To VA, Wisley for C(A) release trials 23/05/58; To A&AEE Boscombe Down for roll/yaw trials 9/06/58; To RAE Bedford on permanent C(A) charge for catapult and arrester development trials 23/07/58; Allocated to RNAY Fleetlands for instruction purposes 25/07/60; To SAH Culdrose 29/10/60; Written off and allocated instructional airframe number A2499 29/11/60; With Air Command Driving School at Culdrose by 1971; To P&EE Shoeburyness 25/11/71 and used for trials up to 3/83; Remains derelict at P&EE 3/88; Fuselage and rear end to Mayer & Perry scrapyard 4/91 and scrapped; Nose section to The Vampire Collection 25/04/91; Loaned to Brooklands Museum 18/07/91, Extant

Specification Number: N.113D
 Contract Number: 6/Acft/6579/CB.7(b) dtd 12/06/51
 Scimitar Prototype
 Quantity: 1
WW134 VA, Hursley Park to A&AEE by road; FF 10/10/56; VA, Wisley for handling trials with flap blowing in operation during flight ; A&AEE 24/10/56; VA, Wisley 2/11/56; RAE Bedford 26/11/56; VA, Wisley 12/56; A&AEE for catapult trials 10/12/56; Aerodrome dummy deck landings 18/12/56; HMS *Ark Royal* for carrier trials 2/01/57; VA, Wisley 7/01/57; Aerodrome dummy deck landings 1/02/57; VA, South Marston for further development work and C(A) release 7/02/57; VA, Wisley by 06/57; C Sqn, A&AEE handling trials for C(A) release 2/07/57; HMS *Ark Royal* for deck landing trials 15/07/5; Measured take-offs and landings, port brake overheating, caused wheel fire, A&AEE, Cat LX 7/08/57; Compressor failure during handling trials under intensive flying conditions, A&AEE, Cat HX 19/08/57; Grounded for repairs; VA, South Marston for further C(A) release trials 17/09/57; C Sqn, A&AEE, tail skid hooked into runway light on arrival, Cat LX 10/04/58; Bird strike, panels of windscreen broken over Bedford airfield, engine damaged 9/07/58; RAE Bedford 22/09/58; A&AEE spinning trials 4/02/59; VA, South Marston de-instrumentation prior to disposal 5/05/59; VA, Wisley, rough runway trials in connection with TSR.2 contract 9/10/59; VA, South Marston & Weybridge for landing trials 14/10/60; VA, Wisley to VA, South Marston in preparation for Anglo-French underwater sink-rate trials 15/03/62; To Trials Officer MoA, St. Mandrier, Toulon, France for Anglo-French underwater sink rate trials 17/06/62; Engines removed and airframe catapulted off *Centaur* into the Mediterranean as part of trials 24/10/62; SOC 2/11/62

Specification Number: N.113D
 Contract Number: 6/Acft/8812/CB.5(b) dtd 11/12/52
 Scimitar F Mk 1
 Quantity: 100 ordered, allocated serial numbers XD212 to XD250, XD264 to XD282 and XD316 to XD357 but cancelled after XD332 (only 76 built)
XD212 FF 11/01/57; Retained by VA, South Marston; To VA, Wisley on C(A) charge for C(A) release 17/04/57; VA, South Marston by 15/05/57; Loaned to the manufacturer by C(A) for display at Paris Air Show 31/05/57-3/06/57; VA, South Marston to VA, Wisley 9/10/57; Failed to respond to controls during take-off, controls locked at point of take-off, engines cut, brakes burnt out and a/c crashed through perimeter fence and ended up in field, hitting lighting post; nose-wheel torn off and leading edge of wing damaged, VA, Wisley, Cat 4 14/10/57; Taken on charge by RN at VA, Wisley 4/06/58; Put on free loan for flight-refuelling trials as receiver 30/06/59 (trials continued on and off until 31/03/61); VA, Wisley to MoS charge 8/10/59; Probe nozzle broke off during

flight-refuelling flight 11/11/59; RAE Bedford for modification and tests of production pylons under catapulting and arresting loads 7/04/60; VA, Wisley 19/04/60; A&AEE for flight-refuelling pod ground trials in blower tunnel 13/05/60; VA, Wisley 16/05/60; Port flap and aileron hit tree top on landing, A&AEE 1/06/60; Repaired on site, still at A&AEE 10/06/60; Failed in-flight refuelling, drogue left attached to probe, fuel spilled over windscreen 17/06/60; Flight-refuelling hose broke away and fell near Lewes, Sussex 21/07/60; VA, Wisley to VA, South Marston 12/08/60; VA, Wisley 31/08/60; Flight-refuelling exercise with XD227, hose severed, rudder and tailplane slightly damaged 27/09/60; VA, South Marston to VA, Wisley 10/11/60; A&AEE 22/11/60; VA, South Marston for trials of streamlined flight-refuelling probe 23/02/61; Removal of instrumentation prior to return to RN charge 30/03/61; VA, Wisley for flight-refuelling trials as receiver 04/61; AHU Lossiemouth on RN charge 12/05/61; No.736 Sqn, Lossiemouth (Code: 614) 5/07/61; Bird strike on starboard wing leading edge after low-level sortie, Cat LQ 14/09/61; Spun in from low altitude while circling contact point during army co-operation exercise, crashed in field on Raich Hill, nr Forres 6 miles east-northeast of Huntly, pilot (Lt T H M Laister) killed, Cat ZZ 20/09/61

XD213 FF 27/04/57; Retained by manufacturer for trials for C(A) release 21/05/57; Attended Paris Air Show 31/05/57-3/06/57; VA, Wisley with detachment to A&AEE for three days 3/06/57; SBAC Air Show, Farnborough 09/57; C Sqn, A&AEE for C(A) release trials and gun firing 25/04/58; RAE Bedford for launching bridle retaining trials 21/11/58; VA, South Marston for mods and inspection 16/02/59; A&AEE for butt firing trials 22/04/59; VA, South Marston to RN charge for modernisation 28/10/59; To Lee-on-Solent, cocooned by MARSTU 6/04/61; AHU, Tengah by sea via RNAY Fleetlands 17/05/61; No.803 Sqn (Code: 152/V) 30/06/61; Starboard engine malfunction on start-up on HMS Victorious, Cat SS 23/02/62; RNAY Fleetlands 30/03/62; Lee-on-Solent by road for flight testing 17/04/62; No.803 Sqn, Lossiemouth (Code: 152/H) 24/06/62; HMS Hermes, probe damaged during in-flight refuelling off Malta, Cat LX 27/06/62; Large bird strike at 3,000ft SW of Crete, landed safely on HMS Hermes, Cat LQ 14/07/62; Drop tank burst during pressure refuelling, HMS Hermes, Cat SS 27/09/62; Bird strike during low-level navigational exercise, Cat LQ 3/01/63; Hydraulic failure after take-off from HMS Hermes, port u/c failed to lower on approach to Yeovilton and a/c was overweight for safe emergency landing, pilot unable to steer a/c out to sea, ejected safely, a/c crashed in field near East Chaldon, Weymouth, Dorset, Cat ZZ 20/09/63; Wreckage to Lee-on-Solent 19/12/63; Still there 17/09/64.

XD214 FF 31/05/57; VA, Wisley to VA, South Marston 13/06/57; VA, Wisley and taken on charge by RN 20/07/57; To C(A) charge at VA, Wisley for C(A) release trials 29/07/57; A&AEE by 09/57; VA, Wisley by 04/58; C Sqn, A&AEE for preparation for tropical trials 9/06/58; Hot weather trials, Bahrein and El Adem 07/58; A&AEE 08/09/58; VA, Wisley for trials 24/09/58; VA, South Marston 24/07/49; For modernisation from 29/10/59; AHU Lossiemouth 1/12/60; No.803 Sqn (Code: 151/V) 16/12/60; Hit by Sea Vixen XJ586 while making a night landing, parked on HMS Victorious, Cat HY 25/01/61; RNAY Fleetlands 26/01/61; To Lee-on-Solent by road for flight testing 8/02/61; VA, South Marston 11/02/61; AHU Lossiemouth 7/11/61; MoA Air Fleet at VA, South Marston for trials installation of Low Altitude Bombing System 8/01/62; AHU Lossiemouth for modifications 30/03/62; No.803 Sqn (Code: 146/V) 17/04/62; Stn Flight, Lossiemouth 20/07/62; Gibraltar via Culdrose 7/08/62; No.803 Sqn (Code: 146/H & 146/R) 8/08/62; False fire warning, diverted to St Mawgan, Cat SS 18/11/62; Bird strike, normal landing, HMS Hermes, Cat LQ 28/12/62; Port throttle jammed during RP attack. Slippery deck, nose-wheel fairing damaged when ship rolled, HMS Hermes, Cat LQ 3/08/63; Starboard hood rail partially detached at start of climb, HMS Hermes, Cat LQ 25/01/64; Took-off from HMS Hermes, fuel transfer problems, diverted to Yeovilton, Cat SS 7/02/64; U/c failed to lock down, used emergency system, landed A&AEE, Cat LQ 22/05/64; Bird strike at 9,000ft, Cat LC 17/06/64; Flaps failed during night landing, emergency selection made, Lossiemouth, Cat LQ 9/11/64; Hydraulic leak while taxiing, Cat LQ 16/11/64; Fuel system malfunction, landed safely, Cat LQ 26/11/64; To Lee-on-Solent 12/01/65; To RNAY Fleetlands by road for modernisation; To Lee-on-Solent by road for flight testing 25/03/66; NASU, Brawdy 17/06/66; Airwork, FRU Hurn (Code: 030 & 830) 17/10/66; nose-wheel collapsed on landing, fire in nose-wheel bay, Yeovilton, Cat HY 28/05/69; To MARTSU Lee-on-Solent by road 17-19/06/69; SOC 23/06/69; Reduced to spares & produce 1/07/69; Still at Lee-on-Solent 26/07/69; To RNAY Fleetlands by road late 1969; Still on RNAY Fleetlands dump 13/06/70.

XD215 FF 06/57; To C(A) loan at VA, South Marston; C Sqn, A&AEE for acceptance trials and Bullpup missile trials 10/07/57; HMS Ark Royal for deck landing trials 15/07/57; VA, South Marston for continuation of C(A) release trials 26/07/57; VA, Wisley 30/09/57;

RAE Bedford for catapult launches and deck gear trials with dart target towing 23/02/59; A&AEE for snatching trials 27/02/59; VA, Wisley with daily visits to A&AEE as necessary 28/04/59; VA, South Marston to VA, Wisley 15/05/59; NAD/RAE Bedford 26/06/59; A&AEE 26/09/59; VA, Wisley 13/07/59; VA, South Marston for modernisation 12/08/59; No.803 Sqn (Code: 150/V & 150/H) 1/02/61; Port compressor blades found to be damaged, HMS Victorious, Cat LY 9/11/61; Brake failure on landing, engaged airfield arrester wire, Yeovilton, Cat LQ 15/03/62; Drifted to port, engaged No.3 wire, port u/c and nose-wheel in catwalk, Cat HY 24/07/62; Shipped to Portsmouth 2/10/62; Lightered via RNAY Fleetlands and by MARSTU to VA, South Marston 8/11/62; No.800 Sqn, Lossiemouth (Code: 108/R) 27/4/63. No.736 Sqn Lossiemouth (Code: 611) 23/06/64; Bird strike at 400ft, Cat LQ 29/07/64; Ricochet damage over Train Range, Cat LQ 30/09/64; Fuel pump problem, landed safely, Cat SS 12/10/64; Hydraulic problem landing, emergency selected, touched down safely, Cat LQ 23/10/64; Bird strike on radome, West Freugh, Cat LQ 28/10/64; Defective u/c warning light, landed safely, Cat LQ 4/11/64; Hydraulic failure, emergency landing, Cat LQ 16/02/65; Access panel lost in flight, Cat LQ 22/03/65; No.764B Sqn (Code: 614) 29/03/65; UHF failure, landed safely; Cat LQ 21/05/65; Faulty compass, Cat LQ 27/05/65; Starboard engine fire warning on take-off, single engine landing, Cat SS 7/07/65; Lee-on-Solent 27/01/66 [last flight]; RNAY Fleetlands by road 28/01/66; HMS Hermes for deck handling training after refit 21/05/66; To Lee-on-Solent by MARTSU for open storage 31/07/66; Dismantled at Lee-on-Solent 2/10/67; SAH, Culdrose by road, GI Class II Instructional Airframe No. A2573 6-9/10/67; Local code SAH-18 allocated but not applied as airframe used by fire section but not burnt 29/11/67; To P&EE Shoeburyness by road 25/11/71 and 1/12/71; Used as ballistic target for gunfire assessment 07/72 to 08/77; Cockpit canopy to RAE Farnborough 24/05/78; Remains part of lot in MoD surplus sale at Shoeburyness; Rear fuselage to Mayer Parry Ltd, Cambs and scrapped 22-26/04/91; Cockpit section bought by Barry Parkhouse/Parkhouse Aviation, Surrey 25/04/91; To Nick Parker for restoration 19/02/94; Extant.

XD216 FF 25/05/57; To C(A) charge at VA, Wisley 25/05/57; A&AEE preliminary handling trials 13/06/57; VA, Wisley 16/06/57; A&AEE for C(A) release trials 12/08/57; VA, Wisley for C(A) release, in-flight refuelling as receiver, Bullpup and TMB trials 5/09/57; Extended pitot head fitted c.1/04/58; A&AEE handling with inboard drop tanks 15/04/58; VA, Wisley 28/04/58; RAE Farnborough to VA, Wisley 18/08/58; Tail cone lost with anti-spin parachute whilst over Lasham 22/10/58; Bird strike, Cat L 9/01/59; VA, South Marston for repair 14/01/59; A&AEE for store handling preview 27/01/59; VA, Wisley for storage 26/02/59; Reflown 8/05/59; A&AEE for pressure error trials 1/07/59; RAE Farnborough for weapons tests 28/08/59; Improved nose fitted 10/09/59; VA, Wisley to NAD Bedford for trials 23/09/59; A&AEE for carrier trials 30/09/59; To HMS Victorious in English Channel for trials 13/10/59; A&AEE 19/10/59; VA, Wisley for re-instrumentation for trials 22/10/59; A&AEE for trials 27/11/59; VA, Wisley; A&AEE 30/12/59; Spinning trials with larger tailplane 18/02/60-7/03/60; A&AEE for drop tank trials 24/03/60; Drop tanks detached and outer and inner pylons torn off due to pitch-up followed by spin, pitot head torn off and underside of mainplanes holed, Cat SS 31/03/60; VA, South Marston for repair 5 or 13/04/60(?); Permanent C(A) charge for trials 14/06/60; Remained at VA, South Marston for engine relight trials 14/10/60-08/61; Tested after repairs 14/11/60; Bullpup and Sidewinder trials from 17/11/60; Top forward and rear sections of tail parachute canister lost in flight 3/02/61; Pressure error trials 25/04/61; NAD/RAE Bedford until 20/12/61; VA, South Marston in preparation for ETPS 7/05/62; ETPS, Farnborough (Code: 22) for student training and lift boundary investigation 28/06/63; Turning test at 30,000ft, electrical failure in spin, pilot recovered at 14,000ft but engines surged and flamed out, pilot (Flight Lt B L Gartner) ejected safely, aircraft crashed in sea 1/2 mile off West Wittering, Sussex, Cat ZZ 16/07/64; Wreck salvaged to AIU Lee-on-Solent; Fuselage and fin remains noted at RNAY Fleetlands 07/67; SOC 19/10/67.

XD217 FF 19/05/57; Retained by manufacturer for test flying and trials; To C(A) charge at VA, South Marston for C(A) release trials 16/08/57; VA, Wisley to C Sqn, A&AEE 11/09/57; Assessed by US Navy test pilots until 27/09/57; Slight damage to fin and rudder after supersonic investigation at high Mach numbers, Cat LQ 18/09/57; VA, Wisley for continuation of C(A) release trials 4/10/57; C Sqn, A&AEE for continuation of C(A) release trials 23/12/57; Rudder damaged as result of violent airframe vibration, Cat LX 21/05/58; VA, Wisley 8/07/58; VA, South Marston 24/04/59; A&AEE for UHF trials 10/05/59; VA, South Marston for checks and trial installation of Violet Picture 25/05/59; VA, Wisley 21/12/59; A&AEE for Violet Picture and radio trials 18/03/60; Failure in port mainwheel lock light, Cat SS 4/04/60; VA, South Marston for modernisation 31/05/60; AHU Lossiemouth 28/02/62;

No.736 Sqn, Lossiemouth (Code: 616) 2/03/63; Fuel vapour in cockpit, precautionary landing, Cat LQ 20/08/62; Tank ruptured on landing, Cat LQ 2/10/62; Bird strike on pull-out over Rosehearty Range, Cat LX 12/07/63; Bird injested into starboard intake, take-off aborted, Cat HY 11/05/64; Oxygen hose problems at 20,000ft, landed safely, Cat SS 27/07/64; Faulty switch, RP fell off into sea off Tain Range, Cat SS 18/03/65; No.746B Sqn, Lossiemouth (Code: 616) 29/03/65; Hydraulic failure on aerodrome dummy deck landing touch-down, Cat LQ 30/03/65; Fuel control problems during night decent, landed safely, Cat SS 13/05/65; U/c warning light malfunction, Cat LQ 24/05/65; To Lee-on-Solent 1/06/65; By road to RNAY Fleetlands for overhaul 2/06/65; Lee-on-Solent for test flying 20/03/67-16/06/67; C Sqn, A&AEE for bomb and low-level camera trials 19/06/67; NASU Brawdy for long term storage 27/03/68; SOC and reduced to scrap 4/09/69.

XD218 FF 05/57; To C(A) charge at VA, Wisley 28/06/57; SBAC show, Farnborugh 1/09/57; VA, Wisley 9/09/57; To temp C(A) charge for catapult trials at RAE Bedford 28/10/58; VA, Wisley 31/10/58; C Sqn, A&AEE for deck landing trials by 05/59; RAE West Freugh 2/06/59; VA, Wisley 2/06/59; RAE West Freugh 18/06/59; VA, Wisley 19/06/59; A&AEE for position error trials 11-13/01/60; VA, Wisley to A&AEE and return 29/01/60; VA, South Marston for tests 22/04/60; VA, Wisley 25/04/60; RAE West Freugh for armament trials 23/05/60; Permanent C(A) charge 14/06/60; RAE Bedford; RAE West Freugh for 2,000lb MC and 25lb practice bomb ballistic trials 1/11/60; RAE Bedford for catapult clearance trials from 30/11/60; RAE Farnborough or West Freugh, as needed for general armament and development trials for 6 months from 10/07/61; VA, Wisley 27/12/61; RAE West Freugh 15-31/01/62; RAE Farnborough 12-15/02/62; RAE West Freugh 19/02/62-16/03/62 and 9-16/04/62; VA, South Marston to Hyeres 19/06/62; VA, Wisley for tests 12/07/62; RAE Farnborough 17/08/62 & 11/09/62; VA, Wisley 13/09/62; RAE West Freugh for armament trials 18/09/62-26/10/62; Temporary transfer to RAE Farnborough or West Freugh for armament trials on a drop-in basis 5-21/12/62; RAE Farnborough to VA, Wisley 21/12/62; RAE Farnborough 1/01/63; VA, Wisley 18/01/63; RAE Farnborough 11 or 15/02/63(?); Starboard engine fire warning, forced landing at Tangmere 18/02/63; RAE West Freugh 22/04/63; VA, Wisley 17/05/63; RAE Farnborough & West Freugh for armament trials 20/05/63; VA, Wisley 11/08/63; RAE Farnborough and West Freugh for armament trials 19/08/63; At Wisley by 09/63; VA, South Marston 25/10/63; Temporary transfer to RAE Farnborough and West Freugh on drop-in basis 1/01/64-1/07/64; Undershot runway on landing, minor damage 30/04/64; VA, South Marston to Weapons Flight, Farnborough for general armament development trials 26/11/64; To RAE West Freugh, bird strike on port engine, Cat LX 3/02/65; To be returned to RN change in exchange for XD228 18/11/66; Damaged during refuelling, Cat 5, early 1967; RNAY Fleetlands by road and sea via Stranraer for long term storage, arrived 20-21/04/67; Allocated to scrap 20/07/67; SOC and broken up 25/10/67.

XD219 FF 2/08/57; To C(A) charge at VA, South Marston for C(A) release trials 16/08/57; A&AEE for C(A) release trials 17/08/57; VA, Hursley Park by road for C(A) release trials then mods and inspection 22/08/57; A&AEE for gunnery trials 4/12/57; VA, Wisley for C(A) release trials 24/02/58; RAE Bedford for arrester gear and catapult trials 23/06/58; VA, Wisley for inspection, preparation for ground engine strain tests and trials installation of *Blue Silk* X-band Doppler navigation radar for flight trials 21/08/58; A&AEE *Blue Silk* trials 28/04/59; VA, South Marston for trial installation and flight testing of nightfighter sight and roller map 22/07/59; A&AEE assessment of nightfighter sight and Spectre camera recorder 26/11/59; Canopy came off while accelerating to climbing speed after take-off, landed safely, Cat LQ 7/07/60; VA, Wisley 28/07/60; VA, South Marston brought up to production standard and instrumentation removed 7/10/60; AHU Lossiemouth 24/05/63; No.736 Sqn, Lossiemouth (Code: 617) 28/06/62; Encountered severe slipstream from other a/c during turn, Cat LQ 24/09/62; Undercarriage indicator malfunction, Cat SS 18/12/62; Starboard u/c warning light malfunction, Cat SS 9/09/63; Starboard u/c warning light malfunction, Cat SS 19/09/63; Hydraulic failure, landed safely, Cat LQ 31/07/64; Flap malfunction at 20,000ft, landed safely, Cat LQ 27/01/65; False instrument reading during RP dives, Cat LQ 12/03/65; Cat SS 18/03/65; RP fired in dispersal, faulty switch, No.764B Sqn, Lossiemouth (Code: 617) 29/03/65; Yeovilton 11/05/65; Lee-on-Solent and RNAY Fleetlands by road 17/05/65; Lee-on-Solent by road for air testing 15/12/66-27/02/67; Airwork, FRU Hurn, but found to be incorrect mod state for FRU use 2/03/67; MTPS, Brawdy 6/03/67; Station Flight, Lossiemouth for static display 9/09/67; Station Flight, Brawdy 11/09/67; NASU, Brawdy 9/01/68; RAE West Freugh 16/02/68; Station Flight, Brawdy 24/05/68; To permanent Ministry of Technology charge at RAE Farnborough 7/11/68; Flown from Brawdy to Farnborough 16/12/68; SOC by RN; Wings chopped for

runway braking/aquaplaning trials with Western Sqn, Farnborough by 03/71; Ran off runway during a high speed run, nose-wheel torn off after hitting runway light and fuselage back broken 21/07/75; Unspecified trials use 07/84-01/86; Fuselage less rear section to fire dump Yeovilton, by road 1/11/90; Tail section was part of MoD sale at P&EE Shoeburyness 4/12/90; Scrapped 04/91; Remainder at Yeovilton scrapped 15/03/94.

XD220 Test flight from VA, South Marston ASI and hydraulic fault, forced landing at A&AEE 12/08/57; VA, South Marston 13/08/57; Delivered to No.700X Sqn, Ford (Code: 800/FD) 11/10/57; Engine fire while trying to relight, extinguishers operated, landed safely, Cat SS 6/03/58; (3/12/57); High tailplane column forces experienced, Cat SS 6/03/58; No.700 Sqn, Ford (Code: 511/FD) for deck landing trials on HMS *Victorious* 23/05/58; No.700 Sqn, Yeovilton (Code: 511/VL) 17/09/58; RNAY Fleetlands 20/02/59; Lee-on-Solent by road for flight testing 31/01/62-13/02/62; No.736 Sqn, Lossiemouth (Code: 618) 15/02/62; Port engine warning light at top of dive over Tain Range, Returned to base, Cat SS 7/03/62; Hydraulic failure while strafing Tain Ranges, landed safely; Cat LQ 16/03/62; Bird strike during low level sortie, Cat LQ 9/04/632; Hydraulic failure, landed safely, Cat SS 16/10/62; Hydraulic failure, emergency landing, Cat SS 13/05/63; Undercarriage problem on landing, Cat LQ 20/05/63; nose-wheel collapsed on start-up, Cat LQ 20/06/63; Hydraulic failure, precautionary landing, Cat SS 27/11/63; Radio failure, Cat SS 10/01/64; Hydraulic failure, emergency landing, Cat SS 22/01/64; Hydraulic failure, precautionary landing, Cat LQ 28/02/64; Undercarriage hydraulic failure, leg freed with + and - G, Cat LQ 4/06/64; Hydraulic failure while landing, Cat LQ 4/08/64; Undercarriage warning light malfunction, landed safely, Cat LQ 10/11/64; Bird strike, starboard intake, Cat HY 18/01/65; No.764B Sqn, Lossiemouth (Code: 621) by 06/65; White smoke from drop tank, landed safely, Cat SS 21/09/65; Undercarriage warning light failure, landed safely, Cat LQ 8/10/65; Bomb fell off on landing, Cat SS 21/10/65; To Lee-on-Solent and on to RNAY Fleetlands by road 27/10/65; To Lee-on-Solent by road for air testing 25/01/68; Aborted take-off, arrested with CHAG gear Lee-on-Solent 27/02/68; NASU, Brawdy for long term storage 21/03/68; Flown to MARTSU Lee-on-Solent for FAA Museum storage 22/02/70; SOC 30/07/70; Dismantled and transported by road to RNAY Wroughton for storage 14/03/73; Exchanged by FAA Museum for USMC F-4 Phantom II; Loaded aboard RFA *Olna* at Portsmouth 2/06/86; Shipped to USA for display on board USS *Intrepid* Air & Space Museum, New York Harbour; Extant.

XD221 FF 20/08/57; Suffered bird strike during test flight, engine damaged, VA, South Marston 21/09/57; Delivered to No.700X Sqn, Ford (Code: 801/FD) 25/09/57; No.700 Sqn, Ford (Code:512/FD) 28/05/58; Temporary C(A) charge at A&AEE for evaluation, setting up, calibration and pilot familiarisation of AII and A55U prior to carrier trials 11/08/58; Returned to No.700 Sqn, Ford 4/09/58; No.700 Sqn, Yeovilton (Code: 512/VL) 17/09/58; To Lee-on-Solent and road to RNAY Fleetlands 10/11/58; At Lee-on-Solent for flight testing by 3/02/61; No.800 Sqn, Lossiemouth (Code: 101/R) 21/02/62; Port ammunition access panel detached on take-off, Cat LQ 2/03/62; Probe damaged when tanker-hose failed to reel in at 30,000ft, HMS *Ark Royal*, Cat LQ 17/06/62; Undercarriage, then Hydraulic 1 failure after take-off from HMS *Ark Royal*, emergency landing on foam-covered airfield, Tengah, Cat HC 3/07/62; AHU, Tengah 17/07/62; No.800 Sqn (Code: 106) 16/10/62; Port tyre burst on landing, Lossiemouth, Cat LQ 6/03/63; While parked, hit by Gannet XP229, Cat LQ 28/05/63; Aborted take-off after rudder malfunction, engaged barrier, Tengah, Cat LC 24/08/63; AHU, Changi 31/08/63; No.803 Sqn (Code: 025/R) 19/01/66; NASU Changi 4/04/66; SOC and reduced to produce and spares 6/06/66; Fuselage dumped at NASU Sembawang 01/67.

XD222 FF 20/09/57; Delivered to No.700X Sqn, Ford (Code: 802/FD) 11/10/57; Used in presentation to RN at Lee-on-Solent 11/11/57; VA, Wisley for overhaul and preparation for winter chamber trials 7/05/58; Minor damage on transfer to Weybridge by road 2/06/58; In cold chamber at Weybridge 5/06/58; VA, Wisley to VA, South Marston to be brought up to production standard 24/12/58; Being air tested from 19/02/60; AHU Lossiemouth 25/03/60; No.736 Sqn, Lossiemouth (Code: 609/LM) 12/04/60; After ground running starboard ECU found to have compressor blade damage, Cat SS 21/09/60. Crashed during low level navigational exercise, Bridge of Cally, 6 miles north of Blairgowrie, Perthshire, pilot (Lt N.J. Norris) killed, Cat ZZ 16/11/60; Wreckage to AIU Lee-on-Solent 1/12/60

XD223 FF 1/01/57; Delivered No.700X Sqn, Ford (Code: 803/FD) 23/10/57; Damaged, Cat LC 28/11/57; No.803 Sqn, Lossiemouth (Code: 803) 29/05/58; PR nose removed 9/09/58; AHU Lossiemouth 12/09/58; VA, South Marston 26/02/59; Air tested 3-28/03/60; AHU Lossiemouth 31/03/60; No.736 Sqn, Lossiemouth (Code: 608/LM) 6/05/60; Starboard engine damaged by bird strike, Cat SS 16/06/60; Hydraulic 1 failure, precautionary landing, Cat SS 15/02/61; nose-wheel collapsed on landing, Cat LQ 28/03/61; Bird hit windscreen at 2,000ft, Cat LQ 25/05/61; Brake binding, port wheel caught fire in dispersal, Cat LQ 21/11/61; Tailpipe fire on start-up, Cat SS 10/01/63; RNAY Fleetlands 21/02/62; To Lee-on-Solent by road for air testing 6/04/63; AHU Lossiemouth 18/04/63; No.800 Sqn (Code: 106/R) 29/04/63; HMS *Ark Royal*, fuel flow problems, diverted to Port Reitz, Cat SS 22/06/63; Fuel flow problems, HMS *Ark Royal*, Cat SS 5/11/63; No.803 Sqn (Code: 156/H) 26/02/64; Bird strike on take-off, Cat LQ 23/03/64; RNAY Fleetlands 5/06/64; To Lee-on-Solent for flight testing 7/07/64-22/08/64; Starboard oil pressure warning, one engine landing, Lossiemouth, Cat HY 9/12/64; Port tyre burst on touch-down, Lossiemouth, Cat LQ 8/01/65; Hood came off during launch, HMS *Ark Royal*, Cat LQ 2/03/65; Mast raised into leading edge of tailplane, HMS *Ark Royal*, Cat LQ 13/07/65; Crashed on final approach following engine problems, pilot (Lt P.A.A. Waring) injured, Changi, Cat ZZ 20/09/55; Remains allocated for fire fighting practice 30/10/65; Wreck at NASU Sembawang by 1966.

XD224 FF 26/10/57; Delivered to No.700X Sqn, Ford (Code: 804/FD) 6/01/58; Cat SS 3/03/58; No.803 Sqd, Lossiemouth 3/06/58; AHU Lossiemouth for storage 17/07/58; No.736 Sqn, Lossiemouth (Code: 618/LM) 27/08/59, Cat SS 23/11/59; Cat LX 30/01/60; By 06/60 was coded 615/LM; Cat LX 23/08/60, To VA, South Marston 4/10/60, VA, Wisley 5/11/60; AHU Lossiemouth 18/07/62' Cat LQ 23/11/62, Cat LQ 26/11/62, Cat SS 2/02/63, Cat SS 7/05/63, Hit XD227, Cat SS 6/08/633, Cat LQ 23/10/63; VA, South Marston 5/03/64; Cat LQ 5/10/64, Cat LQ 7/10/64; Cat LQ 9/10/64, Cat SS 24/10/64, No.764S Sqn, Lossiemouth (Code: 614) 29/03/65, Cat SS 7/04/65, To Lee-on-Solent then RNAY Fleetlands for modernisation 10/06/65; To Lee-on-Solent 19/07/67; Returned to RNAY Fleetlands 10/67; Lightered to HMS *Victorious* 31/10/67; Planned carrier trials cancelled; Returned to RNAY Fleetlands via MARTSU 8/01/68; To NASU Brawdy via Lee-on-Solent 22/01/68; C Sqn, A&AEE Boscombe Down 30/04/68; Released by C(A) from 16/07/69; Sold to Ministry of Technology 12/09/69; At Lee-on-Solent 1970; Arrive P&EE Shoeburyness 23/01/70; Used as ballistic target 04/75-10/79; Wingless fuselage still at P&EE 03/88 believed scrapped shortly afterwards.

XD225 FF 29/11/57; Delivered No.700X Sqn, Ford (Code: 805/FD) 6/01/58, RAE Bedford 7/03/58, Cat 3 17/05/58, No.803 Sqn, Lossiemouth 3/06/58; Landing accident 23/06/58, VA, South Marston by road 13-14/07/58 for repair, refurbishment & modernisation; Air test 29/01/60; AHU Lossiemouth for storage 10/03/60; No.736 Sqn, Lossiemouth (Code: 613/LM) 24/03/60; Cat SS 17/02/61, Cat LX 9/03/61; Cat LQ 14/03/61; Cat LQ 25/04/61; Hit XD240 while landing, Cat LQ 17/11/61; Cat SS 21/11/61; RNAY Fleetlands for modernisation 18/04/62; Towed to Lee-on-Solent by 31/05/63; Final tests at Lee-on-Solent before departure 18/06/63; AHU Lossiemouth 20/06/63; No.803 Sqn (Code: 154/H) 18/06/63; Cat SS en-route to HMS *Ark Royal* 30/11/63; Cat LQ 10/01/64; Code change to 154/R by 28/05/64; Code change to 147/R by 08/64; Cat LQ 15/10/64; Cat LQ 20/01/65; AHU Lossiemouth 01/65; No.736 Sqn. Lossiemouth (Code: 613) 8/02/65; No.764B Sqn, Lossiemouth (Code: 620) 29/03/65; Cat LQ 5/04/65; Cat LQ 15/05/65; Cat SS 4/08/65; Lee-on-Solent 23/11/65; Towed to RNAY Fleetlands for modernisation 29/11/65; Towed to Lee-on-Solent 17/08/66; NASU Brawdy for modifications 31/08/66; Airwork FRU 21/11/66; Lee-on-Solent to await disposal 8/01/69; RAE Farnborough on permanent Ministry of Technology charge 3/02/69; Sold to Ministry of Technology 14/05/69; By road to RNAY Fleetlands for spares recovery 1/09/69; To P&EE Shoeburyness 01/70; Fuselage to Larkhill artillery ranges 8/10/70; Last noted there 5/71.

XD226 FF 20/12/57; To C(A) at VA 6/01/58; A&AEE for Target Towing trials 20/01/58; RNAS Ford 28/02/58; No.700 Sqn, Ford (Code: 510/FD) 12/03/58; A&AEE 7/08/58; Returned to No.700 Sqn, Ford 4/09/58; No.700 Sqn, Yeovilton (Code: 510/VL) 19/09/58; No.764 Sqn, Lossiemouth 11/02/59; No.736 Sqn, Lossiemouth (Code: 610/LM) 12/05/59; RNAY Fleetlands 13/07/59; Departed to Lee-on-Solent 29/07/59; Returned to No.736 Sqn, Lossiemouth (Code: 610/LM) 31/07/59; Cat HX 4/09/59; AHU Lossiemouth for modernisation 27/07/60; VA, South Marston to be brought up to production standard 23/08/60; AHU Lossiemouth 3/11/61; Air Test 12/61; No.736 Sqn, Lossiemouth (Code: 615) 22/01/62; Cat LQ 24/01/62; Cat LQ 15/02/62; Cat SS 23/01/63; Cat HX 9/04/63; AHU Lossiemouth 17/04/63; C(A) loan at VA, South Marston 11/11/63; AHU Lossiemouth 11/03/64; RAF Handling Sqn, Boscombe Down 22/06/64; AHU Lossiemouth 12/08/64; A&AEE on loan 19/07/64; AHU Lossiemouth 12/08/64; To AES Arbroath as Class I GI 7/01/65; Downgraded to Class II as Instructional Airframe No. A2562 27/07/67; Downgraded to Class III 06/69; By road to RAE Farnborough 24/06/70; Presumed scrapped.

XD227 FF 23/12/57; To C(A) charge at VA, South Marston 1/01/58; RAF

Handling Sqn, Boscombe Down 8/01/58; VA, Wisley 19/03/58; VA, South Marston 2/04/58; Drop tank tail cones disintegrated in flight 4/03/59; RAF Handling Sqn, Boscombe Down 1/05/59; VA, Wisley 20/07/59; VA, South Marston 12/08/60; Cat SS 29/08/60; Hose severed during inflight refuelling 27/09/60; A&AEE Boscombe Down Cat 2 22/11/60; Cat LX 12/01/61; Cat LQ 23/01/61; Cat 2 15/03/61; Refuelling hose and drogue damaged 18/04/61; A&AEE Boscombe Down 28/04/61; VA, South Marston for removal of test equipment, modernisation and bringing up to production standard 17/05/61; Free loan for trials of photo-reconnais-sance nose 26/04/62; VA, South Marston 18/05/62; AHU Lossiemouth, taken on RN charge 2/04/63; No.736 Sqn, Lossiemouth (Code: 615) 23/05/63; Cat SS 20/06/63; Taxied into XD224, Cat SS 6/07/63; Cat LX 13/09/63; Cat LX 22/11/63; Cat LQ 3/04/64; Cat LQ 9/06/64; Cat LQ 9/06/64; Cat SS 23/07/64; Cat LQ 2/11/64; Cat LQ 2/12/64; Cat HY 8/01/65; Cat LQ 6/03/65; No.764B Sqn, Lossiemouth (Code: 615) 29/03/65; Cat SS 24/06/65; Cat LQ 8/07/65; Struck lorry during taxiing, Cat LQ 14/07/65; Cat LQ 24/07/65; Cat LQ 18/09/65; To Lee-on-Solent 23/11/65; To RNAY Fleetlands for modernisation 29/11/65; NASU Brawdy for storage 15/03/66; Airwork FRU 6/02/67; NASU Brawdy 6/04/67; Windscreen cracked during air test 13/11/67; Airwork FRU 27/11/67; Retired from use 15/03/69; By road to Ministry of Technology, Farnborough 29-30/07/69; SOC and dismantled for movement to P&EE 15/09/69; Transported to P&EE Shoeburyness 12/11/69; Used for ballistic trials 08/70; Fuselage to Larkhill artillery ranges 18/12/70; Last reported there 05/71.

XD228 FF 31/12/57; To Lee-on-Solent 14/02/58 and by road to RNAY Fleetlands; A&AEE Boscombe Down 20/03/58; No.700X Sqn 24/03/58; RAE Bedford 16/06/58; Returned to A&AEE 26/08/59; VA, Wisley for modifications 14/10/59; VA, South Marston for modifications 4/11/59; West Freugh by 23/01/60; C Sqn, A&AEE Boscombe Down 26/01/60; Cat 2 26/01/61; VA, South Marston for removal of test equipment and refurbishment to production standard 13/03/61; A&AEE to VA, South Marston 3/05/61; Test flown at A&AEE Boscombe Down 16/05/61; AHU Lossiemouth 20/11/62; No.736 Sqn, Lossiemouth (Code: 613) 10/12/62; Cat SS 31/01/63; Cat LQ 27/02/63; Damaged by debris over Tain Ranges, Cat LQ 18/07/63; Cat SS 14/10/63; Bird strike, Cat SS 21/11/63; Cat LQ 24/02/64; Cat SS 12/03/64; Bird strike, Cat LQ 21/07/64; Heavy landing, Cat LQ 13/10/64; A&AEE Boscombe Down 18/03/65; RAE Bedford 23/04/65; To permanent MoA charge 18/11/66; Non-flying hack by 15/02/67; Released 31/03/70; RAE Farnborough and SOC 22/06/70; In derelict state by 03/76; Parts to P&EE Shoeburyness 9, 23 & 31/09/75; Used for ballistic trials from 07/84; Mid-fuselage and engines to P&EE Pendine Ranges 6/07/88; Wings and part fuselage dumped separately at P&EE 03/88; Wings formed lot in MoD sale at P&EE Shoeburyness 4/12/90; Sold for scrap and removed off site by 04/91.

XD229 To C(A) charge at VA, Wisley 28/06/57; A&AEE Boscombe Down 13/03/58; VA, Wisley 10/04/58; Weapons Flight, Farnborough 26/06/58; Transferred from temporary to permanent C(A) charge; Cat 2 12/11/58; Development trials 17/11/59; Damaged in aborted take-off, Farnborough, Cat HC 27/05/60; Bird strike, Cat 2 25/09/61; Cat 1 17/10/61; Cat 1 24/11/61; Flap failure 24/05/62; Instrument failure 22/10/62; Loaned to A&AEE during 1962 then returned to Weapons Flight; RAE West Freugh to VA, South Marston for modifications prior to trials 15/01/62; RAE West Freugh 3/06/65; Weapons Flight, RAE 10/06/65; Damaged on landing 08/65; Ground hydraulics accident 08/66; SOC as spares 12/10/66; On dump at West Freugh by 03/71 to at least 05/75; Being removed for scrap during 06/76: Some parts to RNEC Manadon.

XD230 Test flight VA, South Marston 21/01/58; VA, South Marston for gun firing modifications 28/01/58; No.700X Sqn, RNAS Ford (Code: 805/FD) 26/02/58; Bird strike, Cat SS 3/03/58; Jet pipe fire 13/03/58; No.803 Sqn (Code: 145/V) 27/05/58; AHU Lossiemouth for storage 9/09/58; VA, South Marston brought up to production standard 3/02/59; Air tested 3-23/02/60; AHU Lossiemouth 18/03/60; No.736 Sqn, Lossiemouth (Code: 617/LM) 1/04/60; Damaged over Tain Ranges, Cat SS 6/05/60; Bird strike, Cat LX 27/05/60; Bird strike, Cat SS 16/06/60; Engine fire, Cat LQ 30/08/60; Engine vibrations, Cat SS 28/09/60; Hydraulic failure, Cat SS 11/10/60; RNAY Fleetlands for modernisation 23/05/62; To Lee-on-Solent by 13/09/63; Air test Lee-on-Solent to Boscombe Down 29/07/63; Returned to Lee-on-Solent 2/08/63; Last air test and departed Lee-on-Solent 21/08/63; AHU Lossiemouth 30/09/63; No.803 Sqn (Code: 154/H) 27/02/64; Recoded (Code: 514/R) 05/64; Cat LQ 23/09/64; Hydraulic failure, ditched after undercarriage refused to lower, pilot ejected safely into Moray Firth off Lossiemouth, Cat ZZ 28/09/64; Aircraft recovered and eventually moved to West Freugh, where still used as Instructional Airframe by 1969: Presumed subsequently scrapped.

XD231   FF 27/01/58; No.700X Sqn, Ford (Code: 806/FD) 1/04/58; No.803 Sqn (Code: 152/V) 20/05/58; AHU Lossiemouth for storage 9/09/58; RNAY Fleetlands via Yeovilton 13/11/58; Towed to Lee-on-Solent 31/07/61; Air tested at Boscombe Down 20/07/61; Air tested there until 31/07/61; No.736 Sqn, Lossiemouth (Code: 609/LM) 15/08/61; No.800 Sqn loan to RAE Farnborough for trials, damaged Cat LX 21/08/61; Loaned to No.800 Sqn (Code: 108/R) for SBAC show 09/61; Returned to No.736 Sqn, Lossiemouth (Code: 609/LM) 09/61; VHF failure, Cat SS 19/09/61; Damage over Tain Ranges, Cat HX 6/11/61; Undercarriage malfunction, Cat SS 1/02/62; Damaged on take-off, Cat SS 21/03/62; To Lee-on-Solent 3/04/62; To RNAY Fleetlands 4/04/62; Towed to Lee-on-Solent 15/08/62; Flew to A&AEE Boscombe Down 15/08/62; Flew to AHU Lossiemouth 16/08/62; No.800 Sqn (Code: 101/R) 5/01/63' Hit by XD323 in hangar, Cat LX 5/02/63; Cat SS 27/07/63; Cat LX 27/11/63, Cat SS 14/01/64, Cat SS 24/01/64; Fuel leak, Cat LQ 28/01/64; AHU Lossiemouth 5/02/64; No.800B Flight, Lossiemouth (Code: 111/E) 29/09/64; AHU Lossiemouth 2/10/64; RNAY Fleetlands for rectification 26/10/64; RAE Farnborough 10-11/64; RNAY Fleetlands for fitment of instrumentation 12/64; Allocated to RAE Bedford 12/02/65; Shipped to Oklahoma for tests with NACA & MoA 03/65; Returned to VA, South Marston 31/08/66; RAE Farnborough & West Freugh 08/66; NASU Brawdy by 07/67; Weapons Flight, RAE Farnborough 2/08/67; Returned to Farnborough to be scrapped 25/03/69; Allocated for ejection trials 21/08/69; SOC as Ground Engineering Vehicle 17/06/70; Allocated to P&EE Shoeburyness 16/06/70; Still intact at Farnborough by 07/71 including static display in hangar during 09/74; In sections to P&EE Shoeburyness 4/07/75, 16/07/75, 31/07/75 and 22/09/75; Rear fuselage and jet pipe to Pendine Ranges 6/07/83.

XD232   FF 19/02/58; AHU Lossiemouth 23/04/58; Engine fire, Cat LX 7/05/58; No.803 Sqn (Code: 146/V) 6/06/58; Collision with jet blast deflector on HMS Victorious, Cat LX 3/01/59, Hit by XD264 on Victorious, Cat LX 20/03/59; Cat SS 7/05/59; Hydraulic failure, Lossiemouth, Cat LQ 10/09/59; Hydraulic failure, HMS Victorious, Cat SS 21/09/59, Cat SS 25/01/60; Lee-on-Solent 12/04/60 and onward to RNAY Fleetlands for modernisation; Towed back to Lee-on-Solent 20/06/61; Air tested from Lee-on-Solent to Boscombe Down 26/06/61; Last air test from Lee-on-Solent 11/07/61; AHU Lossiemouth and onwards to VA, South Marston on free loan 20/07/61; A&AEE Boscombe Down 6/09/61; AHU Lossiemouth 9/10/61; Lee-on-Solent for MARTSU 20/10/61; Shipped to Far East on SS Benarty 11/11/61; Arrived Tengah, Singapore 13/12/61; No.807 Sqn (Code: 193/C) 1/02/62; Stn Flight, Lossiemouth 26/04/62; To Lee-on-Solent 15/05/62 and towed to RNAY Fleetlands; Towed back to Lee-on-Solent 21/11/62; Air tested 26/11/62; Hydraulic failure during ferry flight to Lossiemouth, Cat SS 28/11/62; No.736 Sqn, Lossiemouth (Code: 611) 29/11/62; Brake failure, Cat LQ 19/03/63; False undercarriage light, Cat LQ 14/05/63; RNAY Fleetlands 5/06/63; No.736 Sqn, Lossiemouth (Code: 611) 10/07/63; Hydraulic failure, Cat LQ 25/07/63; Hydraulic failure, Cat LQ 3/10/63; Hydraulic failure, Cat SS 4/11/63; Damaged during in-flight refueling, Cat HY 5/06/64; To Lee-on-Solent 10/06/64 and on to RNAY Fleetlands; Towed back to Lee-on-Solent 10/01/66; Departed Lee-on-Solent 02/66; RAE Bedford 17/03/66; NASU Brawdy 12/10/66; Airwork FRU 11/01/67; Sold to Ministry of Technology for P&EE 11/09/67; To Ministry of Technology, Farnborough for scrapping 5/12/69; P&EE Shoeburyness by road 16-18/06/70; Believed finally scrapped and left P&EE Shoeburyness 2/11/83.

XD233   Retained by manufacturer as static test airframe and repeated loaded to stress airframe for a typical low-level sortie. Helped to ascertain that the airframe was good for a fatigue life of 1,000hrs. Tests undertaken in Flight Test Centre at Wisley, presumed eventually scrapped.

XD234   FF 14/04/58; AHU Lossiemouth 2/05/58; No.803 Sqn (Code: 147/V) 30/05/58; Hydraulic failure, Cat SS 2/07/59; Hydraulic failure, Cat SS 17/07/59; Fault while ashore in UK 9/09/59; RNAY Fleetlands via Lee-on-Solent 9/10/59; No.736 Sqn, Lossiemouth (Code: 616/LM) 15/10/59; Single-engine landing, Cat SS 22/07/60; RNAY Fleetlands for modernisation 3/08/60; Air tested, Lee-on-Solent to Boscombe Down 23-24/08/61; AHU Lossiemouth 1/09/61; No.800 Sqn, HMS Ark Royal 16/10/61; Fire damage in dive brake bay, Cat LY 17/10/61; AHU Lossiemouth 22/10/61; RNAY Fleetlands 3/11/61; Lee-on-Solent 21/03/62; Departed Lee-on-Solent 18/04/61; No.803 Sqn (Code: 153/V) 27/04/62; Tailplane hit by XD318, Cat LQ 13/08/62; Bomb fell off in flight, Cat SS 29/11/62; Hydraulic problems, Cat SS 28/05/63; AHU Tengah 05/63; Returned to No.803 Sqn (Code: 153/H) 06/63; Recoded (Code: 153/R) 05/64; Hydraulic failure, Cat LQ 11/01/65; False engine fire warning, Cat SS 8/03/65; Brake failure, Cat SS 1/04/65; Lee-on-Solent 17/05/65 and onward to

RNAY Fleetlands for modernisation; Towed back to Lee-on-Solent 22/02/67; Departed Lee-on-Solent 21/04/67; Airwork FRU 7/04/67; Hydraulic leak, ran off runway, Cat LQ 6/02/69; Sold to Ministry of Technology 30/11/70; Flown from Hurn to Southend Airport 20/01/71; By road to P&EE Shoeburyness 14-15/02/71; By road to RAE Farnborough dump 16/05/74; Did depart Farnborough, but returned and derelict there by 1977; Presumed scrapped.

XD235   FF 25/04/58; AHU Lossiemouth 30/04/58; No.803 Sqn Lossiemouth (Code: 148/V) 7/06/58; Pressure instruments failed on take-off, Cat SS 27/08/59; To Lee-on-Solent 1/09/60 and onwards to RNAY Fleetlands for modernisation; Back to Lee-on-Solent 15/01/62; Departed Lee-on-Solent 16/01/62; No.803 Sqn (Code: 149/V) 19/01/62; Recoded (Code: 149/H) by 04/62; NARIU Lee-on-Solent 29/04/62; RNAY Fleetlands 16/08/62; Departed Lee-on-Solent after air test 27/09/62; No.803 Sqn (Code: 149/H)18/10/62; Unable to release 1,000lb bomb, Cat SS 1/11/62; Tail skid dragged on launch, Cat LC 18/12/62; Engines slow to respond, Cat SS 17/01/64; Recoded (Code: 149/R) 05/64; ASI fault, Cat LQ 24/09/64; Engine failure, Cat LY 28/10/64; Hydraulic failure, Cat LQ 12/01/65; Altimeter fault had to land in formation at Lee-on-Solent 23/02/65; RNAY Fleetlands for modernisation and conversion for FRU duties 25/02/65; Towed to Lee-on-Solent 11/07/66; NASU Brawdy for modifications 31/08/66; Airwork FRU 11/11/66; Fuel problems, Cat SS 26/04/67; Recoded (Code: 032) 10/67 and (Code: 832) 12/68; RAE Farnborough, sold to Ministry of Technology 30/01/70; Flown from Hurn to Southend Airport 16/03/70; P&EE Shoeburyness by road 19-23/03/70; Used for ballistic trials 10/74 - 09/83; Battle damage repair training, RAF Abingdon 12/10/77; Fuselage w/o engines returned to Shoeburyness 25-27/04/78; Lot in MoD sale at Shoeburyness 4/12/90; Fuselage scrapped by Mayer & Perry, Cambs 04/91; Cockpit section acquired by Jeff King; No.424 Sqn ATC & Southampton Hall of Aviation by 1977; Cockpit section to Dave Thomas, Powys 20/02/99; Extant

XD236   FF 22/04/58; AHU Lossiemouth 8/05/58; Acceptance flight 9/05/58; No.803 Sqn (Code: 150/V) 31/05/58; Hydraulic system failure, Cat LX 9/10/58; Unable to lower hook, arrested by emergency barrier (first operational use of this by a Scimitar), Cat HY 20/03/59; RNAY Fleetlands 26/03/59; Air tested Lee-on-Solent to Boscombe Down 9/06/61 until 19/06/61; No.807 Sqn (Code: 195/C) 23/06/61; ERU accidently fired on ground, Cat SS 28/09/61; AHU Tengah 31/01/62; Canopy jettisoned in hangar, Cat LX 28/05/62; No.803 Sqn (Code: 158/H) 1/04/63; Both engines flamed out during taxiing, Cat SS 8/04/63; AHU Tengah 27/06/63; No.800 Sqn (Code: 108) 16/07/63; No.803 Sqn (Code: 158/H) 27/02/64; Recoded (Code: 154/R) 05/64; Bird strike, Cat LQ 12/10/64, Bird strike, Cat LQ 24/10/64; Drogue and hose detached, Cat SS 30/10/64; Bird ingested into engine, Cat HY 11/01/65; To Lee-on-Solent 5/03/65 and towed to RNAY Fleetlands for modernisation and conversion to FRU duties; Towed back to Lee-on-Solent 7/09/66; Air tested Lee-on-Solent to Boscombe Down 16/12/66; Airwork FRU 15/12/66; Hydraulic failure, Cat SS 9/06/67; Hydraulic leak, Cat LQ 14/06/67; Recoded (Code: 038) 10/67; Undercarriage hydraulic fault, Cat LQ 27/11/67; Radio altimeter failure during bad weather exercise with radar picket Corunna, flew into high ground St. Catherines Down, North of St. Catherines Point, Isle of Wight, Pilot (Mr T E Hill) killed, Cat ZZ 26/06/68; Remains to AIU Lee-on-Solent for investigation by 1/07/68; SOC at RNAY Fleetlands 19/03/69; Extant there by 08/69 but scrapped soon afterwards.

XD237   FF 22/04/58; AHU Lossiemouth 20/06/58; Acceptance flight 7/07/58; No.803 Sqn (Code: 149/V) 12/07/58; Rear of jet pipe detached and damaged airframe, diverted to Hal Far, Cat LC 10/12/58; RNAY Fleetlands for repair 22/01/59; Air Test Lee-on-Solent to Boscombe Down 27-28/10/59; AHU Lossiemouth 4/11/59; No.736 Sqn, Lossiemouth (Code: 611/LM) 10/11/59; Wing found to be damaged after bomb release over Tain Ranges, Cat LQ 20/10/60; Tyre burst, Cat LQ 5/06/61; Lost height slowly after dive during army co-operation exercise, hit ground at shallow angle, Grange Farm, 2miles E of Keith, Banffshire, Cat ZZ, pilot (Flt Lt M Farmer, RAF) killed 22/06/61; Written off 2/07/63

XD238   FF 25/04/58; AHU Lossiemouth 20/06/58; Acceptance flight 30/09/58; No.803 Sqn, HMS Victorious (Code: 145/V) 23/10/58; Rocket adaptors and rails jettisoned in error, Cat SS 21/04/59; Holdback ring entered catapult, Cat SS 7/05/59; Tyre burst after brake fire, Cat LQ 14/10/59; Swung and hit refueller while taxiing at Lossiemouth, Cat LQ 12/01/60; Fuel leak during flight from Victorious, engine flamed out during approach to Lossiemouth, pilot (Lt Cdr P.S. Davis) ejected and received slight injuries, aircraft crashed on road near Lossiemouth Golf Course, Cat ZZ 6/02/60; SOC 31/08/60; Wreckage moved to boundary of airfield by 06/64, but gone by 1/07/64 presumed scrapped.

XD239   FF 23/05/58; To C(A) charge at VA, South Marston; AHU Lossiemouth 1/07/58; Acceptance flight 3/07/58 and 19/07/58;

No.803 Sqn (Code: 151/V) 23/07/58; Hydraulic failure and engine fire, Cat SS 12/09/59; Engine fire after relight, single-engine landing, Cat SS 14/09/59; Hit by tug when it skidded on wet deck, HMS *Victorious*, Cat LQ 11/02/60; No.736 Sqn, Lossiemouth (Code: 610/LM) 25/08/60; RNAY Fleetlands for modernisation 7/10/60; Towed to Lee-on-Solent 14/07/61; Departed Lee-on-Solent 31/07/61; AHU Lossiemouth 17/08/61; No.800 Sqn (Code: 109/R) on loan for aerobatic team at SBAC Farnborough 23/08/61; AHU Lossiemouth 12/09/61; RNAY Fleetlands 12/12/61; Controls jammed during air test 17/04/62; Departed Lee-on-Solent 26/04/62; No.736 Sqn, Lossiemouth (Code: 613) 26/04/62; Tyre burst on taxiing, Cat LX 20/06/62; Hydraulic failure, Cat LQ 29/06/62; Hook missed runway wire, Cat SS 22/11/62; Lee-on-Solent 21/01/63; No.800 Sqn (Code: 103/R) 23/01/63; Drogue hit nose, Cat LQ 10/04/63; Undercarriage hydraulic failure, Cat SS 13/05/63; Radio and hydraulic failure during flight from HMS *Ark Royal*, diverted to Khormaksar, failed on first landing attempt due to poor visibility, lost height in turn, pilot (Sqn Ldr C D Legg) ejected and was slightly injured, aircraft ditched in 6ft of water, Aden Harbour, Cat HZ 22/05/63; Wreckage to UK for repair, arrived RNAY Fleetlands 12/07/63; Repair commenced 22/07/63 but stopped due to no funding and airframe set aside for rebuild of XD328; SOC 23/09/64; Remains held at Fleetlands for spares for XD220 until moved to dump 28/04/66; Scrapped at Birmingham Unimetal 03/67.

XD240 FF 23/05/58; AHU Lossiemouth 10/07/58; Acceptance flight 24/07/58; No.803 Sqn (Code: 145/V) 25/07/58; Took part in SBAC show, Farnborough 09/58; Making first landing on newly modernised HMS *Victorious*, pilot caught No.1 wire which pulled out too far and parted, aircraft continued down deck and went off end ahead of ship at walking pace, pilot (Cdr J D Russel) trapped in a/c and drowned, Cat ZZ 25/09/58; Cockpit section recovered from 220ft by the Barfoss and Barnastel off HMS *Reclaim*; Cockpit section to AIU Lee-on-Solent by MARSTU.

XD241 FF 30/06/58; Taken on C(A) charge at VA, South Marston for trials 1/07/58; VA, Weybridge 18/07/58; A&AEE Boscombe Down 5/09/58; RAE Bedford 15/09/58; A&AEE Boscombe Down 21/11/58; AHU Lossiemouth 5/03/59; Acceptance test 1/06/59; No.736 Sqn, Lossiemouth (Code: 614/LM) 3/06/59; Bird strike, Cat SS 19/08/60; Compressor damaged by FOD, Cat SS 16/11/60; Hydraulic failure during landing, Cat LX 1/12/60; Hydraulic failure warning lights, Cat LY 27/02/61; Bird injested into engine, Cat SS 24/05/61; To Lee-on-Solent 15/06/61 and onward to RNAY Fleetlands for modernisation; Towed back to Lee-on-Solent 13/04/62; Lee-on-Solent to Boscombe Down 18/04/62; RAF Handling Squadron, Boscombe Down 25/04/62; AHU Lossiemouth 11/05/62; No.803 Sqn (Code: 150/H) via Culdrose 7/08/62; Engine flamed out, Cat SS 29/10/62; Engine lost power during flight from HMS *Hermes*, landed at Tengah, Cat SS 27/12/62; Compressor failure on take-off, single-engine landing, Cat SS 8/01/63; Nozzle damage during in-flight refuelling, Cat LQ 15/01/63; Panel lost in flight, Cat LQ 4/10/63; Bomb fragments damaged wing over Garvie Island Range, Cat LQ 20/11/63; Recoded (Code: 150/R) 05/64. Windscreen started to break on take-off, Cat LQ 3/11/64; Windscreen cracked in flight, Cat LQ 9/11/64; Flap damaged during dog fight, Cat LX 24/11/64; Engine vibrations, single-engine landing, Cat SS 6/04/65; AHU Lossiemouth 12/05/65; To Lee-on-Solent 5/11/65; With MARSTU by 15/11/65; Towed to RNAY Fleetlands for modernisation and conversion to FRU duties 22/12/65; Towed back to Lee-on-Solent 24/01/68; Departed to NASU Brawdy 22/02/68; Airwork FRU 15/11/68; Hydraulic leak, Cat SS 25/08/69; Transferred to Ministry of Technology charge and flown to Southend Airport 2/12/70; By road to P&EE Shoeburyness 21/12/70; SOC 19/01/71; Used for ballistic trials 11/73 to 01/74; Rear fuselage and jet pipes to P&EE Pendine Ranges 6/07/83; Wings at P&EE Shoeburyness part of lots sold by MoD 4/12/90; Apparently scrapped by 04/91.

XD242 FF 18/06/58; AHU Lossiemouth 24/07/58; Acceptance flight 25/07/58; No.803 Sqn (Code: 152/V) 7/08/58; Hit wire and burst tyre, Cat LQ 6/01/59; Panel lost on take-off, Cat SS 20/02/59; Bird strike, Cat LQ 1/09/59; Attempted single-engine landing, overshot and failed to gain speed or height, wheels-up landing on airfield at Yeovilton, Cat HZ 14/05/60; By road to RNAY Fleetlands 24/06/60; Loaded aboard light and shipped to Scotland; Arrived AES Arbroath 12/07/60; Used as GI Class II Instruction Airframe until 090/64; At MARTSU Lee-on-Solent 01/65 to 05/65; Remains to Aberporth for missile blast-effect trials by 09/67.

XD243 FF 4/07/58; AHU Lossiemouth 1/09/58; Acceptance flight 26/09/58; No.807 Sqn (Code: 190/R) 30/09/58; Hit by crane, Cat HC 10/12/58; Fire warning system operated, Cat SS 14/03/59; Lee-on-Solent by 31/07/59; No.803 Sqn (Code: 147/V) 21/09/59; Slipped on HMS *Victorious* deck, ended up in catwalk, Cat HY 3/02/60; RNAY Fleetlands 26/02/60; VA, South Marston for Cat 4 repairs and modifications 11/04/60; RNAY Fleetlands 19/06/61;

Towed back to Lee-on-Solent 7/07/61; Air test Lee-on-Solent to Boscombe Down 8/07/61; Returned to Lee-on-Solent 28/07/61; AHU Lossiemouth then No.807 Sqn (Code: 191/C) 26/08/61; Pressure instruments failed, landed in formation, Cat SS 6/10/61; No.800 Sqn (Code: 113/R) 27/03/62; Undercarriage malfunction, Cat SS 29/05/62; Speared wire while landing on *Ark Royal*, Cat SS 11/09/62; Flames from exhaust after take-off, diverted to Khormaksar, single-engine landing, Cat SS 17/11/62; Nose probe broke off, Cat LQ 7/03/63; Foreign body entered engine, Cat SS 11/04/63; Bird strike over Tain Range, Cat LQ 18/04/63; Canopy blew off during climb, Cat LQ 1/05//63; Port engine flamed out, landed Embakasi, Cat SS 2/10/63; Hydraulic fault during maintenance at Culdrose, Cat LQ 30/01/64; To Lee-on-Solent 20/02/64 and to RNAY Fleetlands for modernisation; Towed to Lee-on-Solent 21/05/65 and prepared for shipment by MARSTU; Shipped to Far east in *Bacchus* 28/07/65; NASU Changi 10/09/65; No.800B Sqn (Code: 115/E) 21/11/65; Hose loose during in-flight refuelling, Cat SS 20/01/66; Drop tank then hydraulic faults, Cat SS 16/03/66; Damaged by severe turbulence, hail and snow, Cat LQ 15/04/66; In-flight refuelling fault, Cat SS 17/04/66; No.803 Sqn (Code: 025/E) 6/05/66; Tailplane damaged during practice strafing, Cat LQ 15/07/66; Damaged, Cat SS 26/07/66; To GI Class I at AES Lee-on-Solent 24/08/66; Downgraded to GI Class II Instructional Airframe A2588 27/02/68; To RNAY Fleetlands 22/09/70; By road to P&EE Shoeburyness 15-17/01/70; Used for ballistic trials 10/72 to 02/80; Port wing to Farnborough 30/06/76; Port wing returned via No.71 MU 18/11/76; Rear fuselage and jet pipes to P&EE Pendine Ranges 6/07/83; Still there 03/94 presumed scrapped thereafter.

XD244 FF 7/07/58; AHU Lossiemouth 25/08/58; Acceptance flight 15-16/09/58; No.807 Sqn (Code: 191/R) 29/09/58; nose-wheel collapsed on landing at Lossiemouth, Cat HC 29/01/59; No.803 Sqn (Code: 150/V) 16/01/60; No.736 Sqn (Uncoded) 25/08/60; Lee-on-Solent 25/10/60; Towed to RNAY Fleetlands 20/10/60; Air tested Lee-on-Solent to Boscombe Down 27/07/61-1/08/61; Prepared for shipment by sea by MARSTU and shipped to Far East 17/08/61; AHU Tengah 18/09/61; No.803 Sqn (Code: 151/V) 1/10/61; Engine compressor blade damage, Cat LY 3/12/61; To Lee-on-Solent 18/12/61 and onwards to RNAY Fleetlands; Departed Lee-on-Solent 13/01/62; No.803 Sqn (Code: 151/V) 13/01/62; Fuselage hit by tail of XD328, Cat LQ 27/03/62; Recoded (Code: 151/H) 04/62; Tyre burst whilst taxiing, Cat LQ 14/11/62; Smoke from nose during taxiing, Cat LQ 1/01/63: Inflight refuelling probe damaged, Cat LQ 21/02/63; Bird strike, Cat LQ 19/03/63; Damaged by Sea Vixen XJ514 whilst on deck 8/10/63; RNAY Fleetlands for checks and repairs 30/10/63; Departed Lee-on-Solent 24/04/65; AHU Lossiemouth 26/04/65; No.803 Sqn (Code: 153/R) 7/05/65; Engine problem, single-engine landing, Cat LQ 26/05/65; Recoded (Code: 026/R) 07/65; Hose broke off at 1,000ft, Cat SS 31/08/65; Refuelling hose parted, Cat SS 24/09/65; Fire on take-off, single engine landing, Cat HY 31/12/65; Fire warning light, Cat SS 28/01/66; Engine fire warning, single engine landing, Cat SS 7/03/66; Loaned to No.800B Flight 16/03/66; Returned to No.803 Sqn (Code: 026/R) 4/05/66; Bird strike, Cat SS 22/07/66; Hit power cable, landed safely, Cat LX 16/08/66; NASU Brawdy 3/10/66; Air brake fault, Cat LC 6/10/66; To Airwork FRU as reserve aircraft in open storage 3/09/70; Flown to Southend Airport [Last flight of a Scimitar] 12/02/71; By road to Shoeburyness 15/02/71; Sold to Ministry of Technology 24/02/71; Starboard wing to Fort Halstead 23/01/74; Used for ballistic trials 10/74-11/82; Fuselage and port wing to RAE Farnborough 30/06/76; Wing returned via No.71 MU 18/11/76; Fuselage returned via No.71 MU 12/10/77; Remains scrapped by Mayer & Perry scrapyard 04/91; Some parts were obtained by Parkhouse Aviation.

XD245 FF 18/07/58; AHU Lossiemouth 29/08/58; Acceptance flight 3/10/58; No.807 Sqn (Code: 192/R) 4/10/58; nose oleo collapsed, Cat LC 19/08/59; No.803 Sqn (Code: 155/V) 15/01/60; Hydraulic failure, unable to dislodge hook or use emergency system, pilot (Lt R W D Westlake) climbed and ejected at 2,000ft, sadly parachute remained attached to seat and did not deploy, body never found, Cat ZZ 7/02/60.

XD246 FF 29/08/58; AHU Lossiemouth 25/09/58; No.807 Sqn (Code: 193/R) 17/11/58; Fire warning, single-engine landing, Cat SS 19/11/58; RNAY Fleetlands 10/12/58; C Sqn, A&AEE Boscombe Down 19/01/59; No.803 Sqn 5/02/59; Slipped on deck and hit XD264, Cat LY 20/03/59; RNAY Fleetlands 24/03/59; No.803 Sqn (Code: 153/V) 23/04/59; Damaged after bombing over RAE West Freugh, Cat LX 27/04/59; To Lee-on-Solent 4/04/60 and onwards to RNAY Fleetlands; Flown Lee-on-Solent to Boscombe Down 8/09/60; Air tested, Boscombe Down 9/09/60; AHU Lossiemouth 21/09/60; No.800 Sqn (Code: 150/V) 20/10/60; Windscreen shattered over Tarhua Range, Libya, Cat LQ 12/01/61; AHU Hal Far, Malta 16/01/61; To Lee-on-Solent 8/03/61 and onward to RNAY Fleetlands; Air tested, Lee-on-Solent 20/03/61; No.800 Sqn

(Code: 104/R) 22/03/61; No.736 Sqn (Code: 611/LM) 21/09/61; Partial instrument failure, Cat SS 29/09/61; Undercarriage indication fault, Cat LQ 21/03/62; RNAY Fleetlands for maintenance and refurbishment 4/07/62; Back to Lee-on-Solent 3/04/63; Departed to AHU Lossiemouth 5/04/63; No.800 Sqn (Code: 108/R) 16/04/63; AHU Lossiemouth 26/04/63; No.803 Sqn (Code: 152/H) 26/09/63; Damaged over Tain Ranges, Cat LQ 11/03/64; Recoded (Code: 152/R) 05/64; Damaged over Tain Ranges 11/11/64; Flap damaged, Cat LX 27/02/65; To AHU Lossiemouth 04/65; No.764B Sqn (Code: 617) 7/05/65; Port engine fault, single-engine landing Cat SS 29/06/65; Hydraulic problems, Cat LQ 29/07/65; nose-wheel fault after take-off, Cat SS 3/08/65; AHU Lossiemouth 12/08/65; NARIU Lee-on-Solent 29/10/65; Airwork FRU 28/06/66; AHU Brawdy for repair 29/11/66; Airwork FRU 12/12/66; To Lee-on-Solent 20/08/68 and into open storage; Moved by MARTSU to RNAY Fleetlands 29/08/68; To permanent Ministry of Technology charge and moved to P&EE Shoeburyness 8/05/69, arriving 12/05/69; Used for ballistic trails 05/70-05/71; Transported to Larkhill Artillery Ranges for use as a target 05/71.

XD247 FF 26/08/58; AHU Lossiemouth 25/09/58; Acceptance flight 6/10/58; No.807 Sqn (Code: 194/R) 4/11/58; Mid-air explosion, pilot (Sqn Ldr C R Cresswell) ejected but seat did not separate, a/c crashed Cullicudden, Black Isle, Ross & Cromarty, Cat SS 19/08/58; Pilot died of injuries 20/11/58.

XD248 FF 29/09/58; AHU Lossiemouth 31/10/58; Acceptance flight 18/12/58; No.807 Sqn (Code: 195/R) 13/01/59; Engine failure, Cat LQ 12/02/59; Undercarriage fault, Cat SS 2/07/59, Damaged on landing, Cat SS 3/11/59; To Lee-on-Solent 29/01/60; Onwards to RNAY Fleetlands 1/02/60; Flown from Lee-on-Solent to Boscombe Down 16/08/60; Air tested from Boscombe Down 21/08/60; No.803 Sqn (Code: 151/V) 24/08/60; Hydraulic failure onboard, diverted to Lossiemouth, Cat SS 20/10/60; Bird injested, Cat LQ 13/01/61; AHU Lossiemouth 26/01/61; Lost radio contact landed at Henstridge in error, overshot and damaged, Cat:L 12/06/61; RNAY Fleetlands 12/06/61; Air tested from Lee-on-Solent 19/09/61; Loaded aboard SS *Coromandel* by MARSTU for shipment to Far East; Arrived AHU Tengah 6/11/67; No.807 Sqn (Code: 190/C) 1/02/62; Hydraulic failure, engaged barrier, Tengah 7/02/62; Loaded aboard HMS *Centaur* for return to UK 13/02/62; Station Flight, Lossiemouth 26/04/62; Canopy jettisoned in hangar, Cat LX 18/05/62; To Lee-on-Solent 8/06/62; Shipped to Tengah 08/62; Back to RNAY Fleetlands and air-tested Lee-on-Solent 4 & 5/12/62; Departed to AHU Lossiemouth 6/12/62; No.800 Sqn (Code: 102/R) 23/01/62; Bird strike over Dornoch Firth, Cat LQ 30/01/63; Pylon fairing lost in flight, Cat SS 16/02/63; Hydraulic warning, Cat SS 19/02/63; Undercarriage hydraulic failure on take-off, Cat SS 3/04/63; Undercarriage hydraulic fault, emergency landing, Cat SS 10/04/63; Engine damaged, Cat SS 24/06/63; Canopy came off at 32,000ft, Cat LQ 17/01/64; Recoded (Code: 144/R) 05/64; To Lee-on-Solent 6/08/64 and onward to RNAY Fleetlands for modernisation; Towed back to Lee-on-Solent 14/12/65; Technical fault during delivery flight to AHU Lossiemouth, diverted back to Lee-on-Solent 23/02/66; Departed Lee-on-Solent 7/033/66; Returned to Lee-on-Solent for bombing trials 11/03/66; C(A) charge 27/04/66; RNAY Fleetlands to RAE Weapons Flight, West Freugh 12/05/66; Brake failure, Cat LQ 19/01/67; Used as a braking aircraft a/c at Farnborough; NASU Brawdy for removal of instrumentation 17/04/68; Airwork FRU late 1968 but rejected and returned to NASU Brawdy by 22/12/68 for open storage; SOC and RSP 8/07/69; Completely scrapped by 05/70.

XD249 FF 19/09/58; AHU Lossiemouth 30/09/58; Acceptance flight 14/10/58; No.807 Sqn (Code: 196/R) 14/10/58; Bird strike, Cat SS 12/11/58; No.736 Sqn (Code: 612/LM) 15/02/60; Bird strike over Tain Ranges, Cat LQ 20/09/60; C(A) free loan for trials 27/02/61; Returned to No.736 Sqn (Code: 612/LM) 25/03/61; Damaged over Tain Ranges, Cat HX 17/05/61; Hydraulic failure, Cat SS 16/06/61; False fire warning, Cat SS 12/07/61; Failure of undercarriage warning light, Cat SS 4/09/61; Swung on landing, Cat LQ 3/10/61; Lead a/c in landing, overrun b/ 225, wing damaged, Cat LQ 17/11/61; Damaged over Tain Ranges, Cat LQ 23/11/61; To Lee-on-Solent 14/12/61 and on to RNAY Fleetlands; Lee-on-Solent to Boscombe Down 20/09/62; Returned to Lee-on-Solent 24/09/62; Final air test, Lee-on-Solent 3/10/62; To Far east in SS *Ben Wyvis* 6/11/62; AHU Tengah 18/12/62; No.800 Sqn (Code: 111/R) 20/08/63; During ferry flight from Yeovilton ran short of fuel and ditched in Moray Firth after hydraulic failure, pilot (Lt P E H Banfield) ejected but was injured, Cat ZZ 28/01/64; SOC 6/02/64.

XD250 FF 30/09/58; AHU Lossiemouth 28/10/58; Acceptance flight 9/12/58; No.807 Sqn (Code: 197/R)10/12/58; Cat SS 6/2/59; No.803 Sqn 27/01/60; C(A) loan to MoA for Rolls-Royce test of relight characteristics 24/03/60; To Lee-on-Solent and on to RNAY Fleetlands 14/04/60; Towed back to Lee-on-Solent by 4/10/60;

Flown Lee-on-Solent to Boscombe Down 10/10/60; Air Tested Boscombe Down 11/10/60; No.803 Sqn (Code: 150/V) 18/10/60; AHU Lossiemouth 11/01/61; No.800 Sqn (Code: 107/R) 25/03/61; RNAY Fleetlands 3/05/61; Air tested at Lee-on-Solent then delivered to Yeovilton 15/05/61; No.800 Sqn (Code: 107/R) 16/05/61; AHU Lossiemouth 28/11/61; No.736 Sqn (Code: 614) 15/01/62; Fire on start-up, Cat LQ 27/02/62; To Lee-on-Solent 17/08/62 and onwards to RNAY Fleetlands for modernisation (begins) 22/11/62; Flew Lee-on-Solent to Boscombe Down 2/08/63 and 6/08/63; Returned to Lee-on-Solent 7/08/63; Lee-on-Solent to AHU Lossiemouth 10/09/63; No.803 Sqn (Code: 147/H) 31/10/63; Missile fell off at 4,000ft, Cat SS 3/12/63; Recoded (Code: 147/R) 05/64; Single-engine landing, Cat SS 26/06/64; Recoded (Code: 154/R) 08/64 and (Code: 027/R) 07/65; Hydraulic failure, fire in aircraft, ditched in Indian Ocean 30 miles from HMS *Ark Royal*, pilot (Sqn Ldr Z K Skrodzki) unhurt and picked up by No.815 Sqn helicopter 17/02/66.

XD264 FF 28/10/58; AHU Lossiemouth 11/58; Acceptance flight 6/12/58; RNAY Fleetlands 11/12/58; No.803 Sqn (Code: 154/V) 6/02/59; Collided with XD232 on HMS *Victorious*, then hit by XD246, Cat LY 20/03/59; RNAY Fleetlands 25/03/59; No.803 Sqn (Code: 154/V) 23/04/59; single-engine landing, Cat SS 27/04/59; RNAY Fleetlands 13/05/59; Departed Lee-on-Solent 21/05/59; No.803 Sqn (Code: 154/V) 15/06/59; Canopy jettisoned HMS *Victorious*, Cat SS 22/07/59; Canopy blew off over West Freugh, Cat LX 28/08/59; RNAY Fleetlands 12/04/60; Flown to Boscombe Down 20/12/60; Air tested Boscombe Down 3/01/61; No.736 Sqn (Code: 609/LM)10/01/61; To Lee-on-Solent and on to RNAY Fleetlands 28/03/61; Air tested from Lee-on-Solent then on to Boscombe Down 17/04/61; Hydraulic failure during taxi at RAE Bedford, Cat SS 11/07/61; Warning light, landed safely, Cat SS 12/07/61; No.800 Sqn (Code: 108/R) 13/07/61; Hydraulic failure, pilot (Lt Cdr D.P. Norman, minor injuries) ejected 6 miles out over sea but a/c turned and crashed 5 miles South of Cullen, Morayshire, Cat ZZ 21/07/61; WOC 24/07/61; Wreckage to AHU Lossiemouth, then to Staravia at Fleet 12/63; Finally disposed of 12/65.

XD265 FF 20/11/58; C(A) charge at VA South Marston 19/12/58; Returned to RN at South Marston and brought up to RN standard 06/59; AHU Lossiemouth 31/07/59; Acceptance flight 24/08/59; No.800 Sqn (Code: 105/R) 26/08/59; Fire warning light, Cat SS 19/09/59; No.1 hydraulic failure, Cat SS 15/12/59; AHU Lossiemouth 3/05/61; No.800 Sqn (Code: 105/R) 18/05/61; To Lee-on-Solent 18/09/61 and on to RNAY Fleetlands for modernisation; AHU Lossiemouth 25/04/62; No.736 Sqn (Code: 611) 20/06/62; Bird injested into engine during low-level flight, a/c crashed in Moray Firth near Miltown, pilot (Lt Cdr J F Kennett) ejected and recovered by RAF Leuchars SAR helicopter, Cat ZZ 15/11/62; Wreckage dumped at Arbroath and scrapped by early to mid-1963.

XD266 FF 14/12/58; AHU Lossiemouth 19/02/59; Acceptance flight 23/02/59; No.803 Sqn (Code: 155/V) 12/04/59; AHU Lossiemouth 29/05/59; No.803 Sqn (Code: 155/V) 20/06/59; To VA South Marston on C(A) charge 1/10/59; A&AEE Boscombe Down 5/10/59; Damaged during night catapult launch, Cat LQ 15/10/59; Arrester wire parted on landing, went over side of HMS *Victorious*, pilot (Lt J B Cross) escaped unhurt and was picked up by SAR helicopter, Cat ZZ 19/11/59.

XD267 FF 12/12/58; AHU Lossiemouth 11/02/59; Acceptance flight 5/03/59; No.807 Sqn (Code 193/R) 13/03/59; RNAY Fleetlands 9/10/59; Flown Lee-on-Solent to Boscombe Down 4/02/60; Last air test at Boscombe Down 8/02/60; No.807 Sqn (Uncoded) 11/02/60; No.804 Sqn (Code: 164/H) 23/02/60; AHU Lossiemouth 5/05/60; Temporary loan to No.803 Sqn (Code: 155/V) 1/09/60; No.736 Sqn (Code: 610/LM) 6/10/60; Relight test on free loan to C(A) 3/02/61-25/03/61; RNAY Fleetlands 29/03/61; Air tested Lee-on-Solent 18/04/61; No.736 Sqn (Code: 610/LM) 18/04/61; Damaged over Tain Ranges, Cat HX 18/05/61; Impact damage to tailplane, Cat LQ 23/01/62; Hydraulic failure over Tain Ranges, Cat LQ 5/04/62; To Lee-on-Solent 2/07/62 and on to RNAY Fleetlands for modernisation; Returned to Lee-on-Solent by 21/04/63; Lee-on-Solent to Boscombe Down 1/05/63; Last air test and depart Lee-on-Solent to AHU Lossiemouth 3/05/63; No.803 Sqn (Code: 151/H) 4/11/63; Half pylon found missing on landing, Cat SS 12/11/63; Flight refuelling problems, Cat SS 6/12/63; Throttle problem during inverted flight, Cat SS 8/01/64; Recoded (Code: 151/R) 05/64; Panel fell off on take-off, Cat LQ 16/07/64; Canopy lost over sea, landed safely, Cat LQ 21/09/64; Panel lost, Cat LQ 12/11/64; ASI problems, Cat LQ 30/11/64; AHU Lossiemouth 9/02/65; No.764B Sqn (Code: 617) 20/07/65; Warning light malfunction, Cat SS 9/09/65; Refuelling probe head broke off, Cat LQ 13/10/65; Airwork FRU Hurn for pilot familiarisation 1/12/65; NASU Brawdy 21/11/66; Airwork FRU Hurn 18/09/68; Recoded (Code: 835) 12/68; Warning light on take-off, wing tanks jettisoned, landed safely, Cat SS 6/02/69; Sold to

Ministry of Technology for AWRE Foulness 11/09/69; RAE Farnborough for apprentice training 17/10/69; To P&EE Shoeburyness 15-16/09/70; Used for ballistic trials 05/71 to 07/84; Part of port inner wing to Shellmex, Stanlow 8/06/71; Port outer wing to Poton Island 17/05/71; All scrapped by 1984.

XD268 FF 19/12/58; AHU Lossiemouth 17/02/59; Acceptance flight 19/02/59; No.807 Sqn (Code: 194/R) 4/03/59; To Lee-on-Solent 11/06/59; Set fastest overall time in Daily Mail Paris to London Bleriot Anniversary Race, pilot Cdr I H F Martin 15/07/59; RNAY Fleetlands 9/10/59; Air test Lee-on-Solent to Boscombe Down 23/02/60; No.804 Sqn (Code: 165/H) 27/02/60; AHU Lossiemouth 14/05/60; No.803 Sqn (Code: 156/V) 21/06/60; VA South Marston on free loan 27/10/60; A&AEE Boscombe Down for Bullpup and Sidewinder trials 21/03/61; VA South Marston 10/05/61; A&AEE Boscombe Down 21/05/61; RAE Bedford for catapult trials with Sidewinders installed 29/05/61; VA South Marston 30/06/61; A&AEE Boscombe Down for further Sidewinder trials 11/07/61; VA South Marston 17/07/61; A&AEE Boscombe Down for Bullpup trials 30/08/61; VA South Marston 27/09/62; RNAY Fleetlands for modernisation 21/11/62; To Lee-on-Solent 31/01/64 and returned to RNAY Fleetlands; Departed Lee-on-Solent 8/09/64; AHU Lossiemouth 15/09/64; No.800B Sqn (Code: 112/E) 15/09/64; ASI failure, Cat SS 5/11/64; During practice single engine circuit a/c experienced longitudinal instability and insufficient thrust to get out of trouble, pilot (Sqn Ldr A C Hill) ejected and a/c crashed 2 miles short of runway near Duffus, Aberfoyle, Perthshire, Cat ZZ 15/07/65; Remains sold to Messrs Gordon Wilkinson, Elgin, Morayshire 26/01/66; SOC 10/02/66.

XD269 FF 22/12/58; AHU Lossiemouth 4/03/59; Acceptance flight 6/03/59; No.803 Sqn (Uncoded) 10/04/59; AHU Lossiemouth 30/04/59; No.807 Sqn (Code: 195/R) 13/06/59; Panel lost in flight, Cat SS 26/06/59; No.803 Sqn (Code: 156/V) 29/06/59; RNAY Fleetlands for mods and refurbishment 18/12/59; Air tested from Boscombe Down 3-7/04/60; No.803 Sqn (Code: N/K) 8/04/60; Recoded (Code: 147/V) by 05/60; To Lee-on-Solent 25/07/60 and towed to RNAY Fleetlands for mods; Flown Lee-on-Solent to Boscombe Down 26/10/60; Air tested Boscombe Down until 8/11/60; Flown to Yeovilton 8/11/60; Allocated to No.803 Sqn but cancelled 8/11/60; Hal far 15/11/60; Tengah 30/12/60; No.803 Sqn (Code: 151/V) 24/04/61; Starboard brakes failed on taxiing out to catapult, continued and went over side of HMS *Victorious*, pilot (Lt D S Mcintyre) unhurt and rescued by SAR helicopter, Cat ZZ 9/07/61.

XD270 FF 4/12/58; AHU Lossiemouth 8/2/59; Acceptance flight 10/2/59; No.803 Sqn (Code: 149/V) 11/2/59; Hydraulic failure, Cat LQ 10/11/59; RNAY Fleetlands 12/12/59; Flew Lee-on-Solent to Boscombe Down and air tested 7/04/60; No.807 Sqn (Code: 191/C) 14/04/60; Engine fire, single-engine landing, Cat SS 5/08/60; Undercarriage fault, Cat LQ 17/11/60; Ricochet damage over Tain Ranges, Cat LQ 24/03/61; To Lee-on-Solent 28/08/61 and onward to RNAY Fleetlands 27/08/61; Returned to Lee-on-Solent by 9/03/62; Flew Lee-on-Solent to Boscombe Down 12/03/62 and returned; Departed Lee-on-Solent to Yeovilton 15/03/62; No.800 Sqn (Code: 106/R) 19/03/62; Bird strike, Cat HY 7/06/62; Damaged by ricochet over China Rock Range, Cat HY 24/07/62; AHU Tengah 28/07/62; Shipped to UK then to VA South Marston by road 15/11/62; No.800 Sqn (Code: 107/R) 2/05/63; Bird strike, Cat SS 4/05/63; Missile detached on landing aboard HMS *Ark Royal*, Cat SS 6/07/63; Damaged over Ulu Tiram Ranges, Cat LQ 21/08/63; AHU Lossiemouth 13/02/64; No.800B Sqn (Code: 113/E) 18/09/64; Hydraulic failure, Cat LQ 6/11/64; Warning light failure, Cat LQ 17/11/64; Suffered double flame-out in Aden area, pilot (Lt I P F Meiklejohn) ejected safely, Cat ZZ 27/04/65.

XD271 FF 23/02/59; AHU Lossiemouth 13/03/59; Acceptance flight 16/03/59; No.803 Sqn (Code: 150/V) 27/04/59; Cover detached in flight, Cat SS 21/10/59; RNAY Fleetlands 22/01/60; Flown Lee-on-Solent to Boscombe Down 4/05/60; Air tested Boscombe Down 6/05/60; No.803 Sqn (Code: 149/V) 9/05/60; Practice bomb carrier fell off in flight, Cat SS 28/06/60; To Lee-on-Solent 25/07/60 and on to RNAY Fleetlands for modifications; Lee-on-Solent to Boscombe Down and air tested *en route* 18/10/60; No.803 Sqn (Code: 149/V) 18/10/60; ASI failure, Cat SS 26/10/60; Port brake failed, swung into XD328 on HMS *Victorious*, Cat LQ 28/08/61; By lighter from HMS *Victorious* in Portsmouth harbour then to RNAY Fleetlands for modernisation 18/12/61; Lee-on-Solent 25/02/63; Air tested Lee-on-Solent 27/02/63; Electrical fault, Cat SS 22/04/63; Single-engine landing, Cat SS 14/05/63; No.803 Sqn (Code: 155/R) 2/02/64; Hydraulic failure, Cat LQ 15/10/64; nose-wheel fault, Cat LQ 3/11/64; Recoded (Code: 030/R) 07/65; Part of drop tank fell off on catapult, Cat SS 5/08/65; NASU Changi 12/08/65; No.803 Sqn (Code: 030/R) 17/09/65; Smoke in cockpit, landed safely, Cat LQ 22/04/66; NASU Changi 27/04/66; No.800B Sqn (Code: 117/E) 8/07/66; RNAS Yeovilton 15/08/66; To Class I GI at Lee-on-Solent

14/09/66; Downgraded to Class II Instructional Airframe A2589 27/02/68; RNAY Fleetlands for de-instrumentation 14/09/70; Transferred to MOD(Air) and by road to P&EE Shoeburyness 24-25/09/70; Fuselage to P&EE Pendine Ranges 15/09/71; Remainder used for ballistic trials 01/72 to 09/84; Scrapped 09/84.

XD272 FF 23/01/59; AHU Lossiemouth 25/03/59; Acceptance flight 13/04/59; No.736 Sqn (Code: 611/LM) 11/05/59; Bird strike, Cat LX 22/07/59; RNAY Fleetlands 29/10/59; Towed back to Lee-on-Solent by 29/02/60; Lee-on-Solent to Boscombe Down 2/03/60; Air tested Boscombe Down 8/02/60; No.804 Sqn (Code: 166/H) 18/03/60; RNAY Fleetlands 11/04/60; Lee-on-Solent to Boscombe Down and air tested the same day 18/05/60; Collided with Sea Vixen XJ556 while taxiing on HMS *Hermes*, Cat SS 17/08/60; RNAY Fleetlands 1/05/61; No.804 Sqn (Code: 166/H) 05/61; FOD damage to engine, Cat LY 10/08/61; No.800 Sqn (Code: 102/R) 15/09/61; Drop tank transfer failure, Cat SS 18/06/63; To Lee-on-Solent and on to RNAY Fleetlands for modernisation 28/01/63; Towed back to Lee-on-Solent, last noted there 17/06/64; AHU Lossiemouth 26/06/64; No.803 Sqn (Code: 149/R) 14/12/64; Engine flame-out on overshoot, Cat SS 12/01/65; Fire warning light, landed safely, Cat LQ 13/01/65; Engine vibrations, landed safely, Cat SS 5/03/65; False fire warning light over Tain Ranges, Cat LQ 26/03/65; ASI and Machmeter problems, Cat LQ 12/04/65; Recoded (Code: 022/R) 07/65; nose-wheel retraction problem, Cat LQ 8/03/66; Premature bomb release over Tain Ranges, Cat SS 10/08/66; AHU Lossiemouth 1/10/66; RAE Bedford for arrester gear trials 10/66; To GI Class I at AES Arbroath 8/11/66; Downgraded to GI Class II Instructional Airframes A2585 5/03/68; Downgraded to GI Class III 06/69; Presumed scrapped when Arbroath closed 31/03/71.

XD273 FF 27/02/59; AHU Lossiemouth 19/03/59; Panel detached during acceptance flight, Cat SS 20/03/59; No.736 Sqn (Code: 612/LM) 12/05/59; Port undercarriage fairing detached in flight, Cat LX 21/09/59; Fire due to fuel lines being severed after starter disintegration, Cat HY 22/10/59; RNAY Fleetlands for Cat 4 repairs 16/11/59; Lee-on-Solent to Boscombe Down and air tested there 15/08/60; No.803 Sqn (Code: 152/V) 15/08/60; FOD damage, Cat SS 9/02/61; ERU fired in error, Cat SS 22/03/61; Fire warning after pull-out, unable to cancel, climbed to 4,000ft and pilot (Lt G C Edwards - injured in ejection, died at Changi hospital 3/05/61), Cat ZZ 27/04/61.

XD274 FF 19/03/59; AHU Lossiemouth 1/04/59; Acceptance flight 13/04/59; No.736 Sqn (Code: 613/LM) 19/05/59; Temp loan to No.807 Sqn (Code: 198/R) for SBAC show 09/59; RNAY Fleetlands 24/11/59; Lee-on-Solent 28/04/60 Lee-on-Solent to Boscombe Down 2/05/60; Air tested Boscombe Down 3/05/60; No.804 Sqn (Code: 164/H) 7/05/60; Throttle jammed, single-engine landing, Cat SS 1/09/60; Engine damage, Cat SS 9/05/60; Main wheel tyres burst on landing on HMS *Hermes*, Cat LQ 18/09/60; Panel detached during ground-run, Cat LQ 16/02/61; Lee-on-Solent 1/05/61 and on to RNAY Fleetlands; Departed Lee-on-Solent 30/06/61; No.800 Sqn (Code: 104/R) 15/09/61; Smoke from wheel bay, Cat HY 27/06/62; AHU Tengah 25/07/62; Lee-on-Solent 24/09/62 and on to RNAY Fleetlands for repairs and mods; Depart Lee-on-Solent to AHU Lossiemouth 20/03/64; No.800B Sqn (Code: 114/E) 2/09/64; Electrical fault, Cat LQ 4/11/64; Refuelling hose separated from pod and struck Buccaneer, Cat SS 20/01/65; Hose fault during in-flight refuelling, Cat SS 3/02/65; Port aileron hit wire on landing HMS *Eagle*, Cat LQ 18/03/65; Hose parted while in-flight refuelling, Cat SS 20/05/65; Starboard outer drop tank lost in flight 11/11/65; In-flight refuelling hose lost in flight, Cat SS 9/03/66; No.803 Sqn 6/5/66 (Code 024) marked 'EMPTY'; nose-wheel lock failed, Cat SS 1/06/66; Hydraulic failure over Tain Ranges, Cat LQ 15/07/66; To Class I GI at AES Arbroath 2/08/66; Downgraded to GI Class II Instructional Airframe A2584 5/03/68; Presumed scrapped there when Arbroath closed 31/03/71.

XD275 Production test flight 20/07/59; To C(A) charge 15/07/59; Delivered to A&AEE for pre-tropical trials 20/07/59; Tropical trials at RAF Idris 08-09/59; VA South Marston for removal of trials equipment and return to RN 24/09/59; Delivered AHU Lossiemouth 1/02/60; No.803 Sqn (Code: 146/V) 12/07/60; Cat HC, HMS *Hermes* 26/09/60; A&AEE Boscombe Down awaiting collection by RNAY Fleetlands 7/10/60; RNAS Lee-on-Solent 27/10/60; RNAY Fleetlands for repairs 28/10/60; RNAY Fleetlands to A&AEE Boscombe Down for air test 4/01/61; No.803 Sqn (Code: 146/V) 11/01/61; Single-engine landing due to severe vibrations in flight; Returned to RNAY Fleetlands, then air tested and delivered to RNAS Yeovilton 10/05/61; Cat SS, HMS *Victorious* in Lyme Bay 6/02/62; Cat SS, HMS *Victorious* 15/03/62; RNAY Fleetlands for modernisation 30/03/62; RNAS Lee-on-Solent 21/02/63; Departed Lee-on-Solent 22/02/63; AHU Lossiemouth 25/02/63; VA South Marston on free loan to C(A) 2/04/63; AHU Lossiemouth 28/05/63; Temporary to No.736 Sqn,

Lossiemouth 28/06/63; Cat LQ 25/07/63; Noise suppressor trials at RNAS Yeovilton 07-08/633; AHU Lossiemouth 12/08/63; No.803 Sqn (Code: 148/H) 20/09/63; Cat LQ 20/09/63; Struck barrier on HMS *Hermes* 2/01/64; Cat LQ, HMS *Hermes* 6/01/65; RNAY Fleetlands; Towed to RNAS Lee-on-Solent 5/07/65; Brake failure whilst taxiing 14/07/65; Departed RNAS Lee-on-Solent 11/08/65; No.800B Flight (Code: 117/E) 12/08/65; Cat SS, HMS *Eagle* 27/03/66; RNAS Yeovilton 15/08/66; AES Lee-on Solent as GI Class I; Downgraded to Class II Instruction Airframe No.A2587 22/08/67; SOC 27/02/68; By road to RNAY Fleetlands 21/09/70; Transferred to MoD(Air) and moved to P&EE Shoeburyness by road 9/09/70; Last seen on RAE West Freugh dump in 1972, presumed scrapped there at later date.

XD276 FF 28/05/59; AHU Lossiemouth 30/06/59; No.800 Sqn (Code: 100/R) 11/07/59; Cat LQ, HMS *Ark Royal* 29/08/60; RNAY Fleetlands 28/04/61; No.800 Sqn (Code: 100/R) 11/05/61; Cat SS, Lossiemouth 12/08/61; Cat LX, HMS *Ark Royal* 13/12/61; Cat SS 3/09/62; To RNAS Lee-on-Solent 21/12/62; RNAY Fleetlands for modernisation 27/12/62; RNAS Lee-on-Solent by 20/12/63; Cat SS, Lee-on-Solent 28/01/64; NAS Yeovilton 5/02/64; No.803 Sqn (Code: 146/R); Cat LQ, Lossiemouth 9/12/64; Recoded (017/R) 07/65; Cat SS, Lossiemouth 7/08/65; Cat SS, HMS *Ark Royal* 12/10/65; Cat LQ 12/11/65;Cat LQ, Butterworth 12/11/65; RNAS Yeovilton as last operational Scimitar flight from HMS *Ark Royal* 1/10/66; To GI Class I at Lee-on-Solent 21/10/66; Downgraded to Class II Instruction Airframe No.A2591 27/02/68; RNAY Fleetlands by road 23/09/70; Trans to MoD(Air) and to P&EE Shoeburyness by road 21/09/70; To P&EE Pendine Ranges 18/08/71; Fuselage remains scrapped by 05/94.

XD277 FF 02/59; Production test flight 29/05/59; A&AEE Boscombe Down 05-06/59; AHU Lossiemouth 24/06/59; Acceptance test flight 25/06/59; No.800 Sqn, Lossiemouth (Code: 101/R) 3/07/59; Cat LQ, Cottesmore 19/09/59; Cat HX, RAE West Freugh 19/10/59; RNAY Fleetlands 29/01/60; No.800 Sqn (Code: 101/R) 4/03/60; To RNAS Lee-on-Solent 8/03/61; RNAY Fleetlands 9/03/61; Air tested Lee-on-Solent then delivered to RNAS Yeovilton 21/03/61; No.800 Sqn (Code: 101/R) 22/03/61; Cat LQ, RNAS Yeovilton 17/05/61; Cat SS, Munxar Ranges 18/12/61; Cat SS, RNAS Lossiemouth 7/02/62; Cat SS, RNAS Lossiemouth 27/02/62; Recoded (Code: 107/R) during 1962; Cat LQ, HMS *Ark Royal* 15/05/62; Cat HY, HMS *Ark Royal* 17/10/62; AHU Tengah 22/10/62; Shipped to UK; RNAY Fleetlands for repairs 7/01/63; Departed RNAS Lee-on-Solent for Lossiemouth 19/08/64; No.800B Sqn (Code: 111/R) 26/10/64; Cat LQ, Tengah 21/01/65; Recoded during 1965 (Code: 115/E); Cat SS, Lossiemouth 28/07/65, Cat SS, Lossiemouth 10/08/65; Cat LY, HMS *Eagle* 2/09/65; To RNAS Lee-on-Solent 14/09/65; To RNAY Fleetlands until 27/09/65; AHU Lossiemouth 1/10/65; A&AEE for EMC trials 5/10/65; To MARTSU Lee-on-Solent for preparation for shipment 15/10/65; Shipped to Far East 15/11/65; Arrived NASU Changi 12/65; No.803 Sqn (Code: 115/E) 31/03/66; Hydraulic failure followed by both engines after take-off, pilot headed out to sea and ejected (Lt P G De Souza injured), a/c crashed in sea, Cat ZZ 6/04/66; SOC 11/05/66; Large sections were illegally salvaged by Chinese and brought ashore to be sold as scrap, thus hindering any investigation into the cause of the crash.

XD278 FF 15/06/59; AHU Lossiemouth 26/06/59; Acceptance flight 6/07/59; No.800 Sqn (Code: 102/R) 7/07/59; RNAY Fleetlands 29/02/60; Flown from Lee-on-Solent to Boscombe Down and air tested the same day 1/03/60; No.800 Sqn (Code: 102/R) 4/03/60; Abbotsinch 7/03/61; No.800 Sqn (Code: 108/R) 24/03/61; Cat LX, Yeovilton 22/11/61; Cat SS, Yeovilton 14/02/62; Cat LC, HMS *Ark Royal* 28/06/62; Cat HC, Tengah 1/08/62; AHU Tengah 9/08/62; RNAY Fleetlands for repairs and modernisation 24/09/62; Lee-on-Solent to Boscombe Down 1/11/63; Returned to RNAS Lee-on-Solent 8/11/63; Departed RNAS Lee-on-Solent 2/12/63; AHU Lossiemouth 4/12/63; No.803 Sqn (Code: 145/H) 3/02/64; Cat SS, Lossiemouth 15/05/64; Recoded (Code: 145/R) during 1964; Cat LQ 14/07/64; Cat SS, RNAS Yeovilton 2/12/64; Cat SS 11/01/65; Cat LQ 5/04/65; Recoded (Code: 016/R) 07/65; Cat LQ 24/09/65; Cat SS 8/03/66; AHU Lossiemouth 3/10/66; To GI Class I at AES Arbroath 3/11/66; Downgraded to Class II Instructional Airframe A2586 5/03/68; Presumed scrapped when Arbroath closed 31/03/71

XD279 FF 22/06/59; AHU Lossiemouth 3/07/59; Acceptance flight 11/07/59; No.800 Sqn (Code: 103/R) 13/07/59; Cat SS, HMS *Ark Royal* 23/04/60; Cat LY, Hal Far 8/11/60; Ferried back to UK 18/11/60; RNAS Lee-on-Solent 1/12/60 and on to RNAY Fleetlands; Flown from Lee-on-Solent to Boscombe Down 4/01/61; Air tested at Boscombe Down 6/01/61; No.800 Sqn (Code: 104/R) 10/01/61; Damaged 12/01/61; VA South Marston for installation of smoke generating equipment 27/02/61; No.800 Sqn (Code: 104/R) 19/04/61; Cat SS 26/09/61; Damaged, HMS *Ark Royal* 13/11/62; Cat SS, HMS *Ark Royal* 7/12/62; Cat LQ 24/01/63; RNAY Fleetlands for modernisation 21/02/63; Departed

RNAS Lee-on-Solent to AHU Lossiemouth 14/04/64; No.803 Sqn (Code: 143/R) 10/08/64; Cat LQ 16/11/64; Cat SS, Lossiemouth 7/12/64; Recoded (Code: 159/R) 05/65; Recoded (Code: 034/R) 07/65; Cat HY, HMS *Ark Royal* 1/01/66; NASU Changi 27/01/66; RSP; SOC 6/06/66; Remains dumped at NASU Sembawang.

XD280 FF 5/07/59; AHU Lossiemouth 23/07/59; Acceptance flight 20/08/59; No.800 Sqn (Code: 104/R) 21/08/59; Cat SS, Lossiemouth 15/12/59; Cat HY, HMS *Ark Royal* 28/04/60; AHU Hal Far 2/05/60; RNAY Fleetlands 29/07/60; Air tested RNAS Lee-on-Solent 17/04/61; Returned to RNAY Fleetlands for repairs 13/04/61; Flew Lee-on-Solent to Boscombe Down 15/05/62; Last air test (18/05/62) and departed to AHU Lossiemouth 24/05/62; Returned to RNAY Fleetlands Flight Test section for preparation for shipment by MARTSU 8/06/62; Arrived Far East 29/07/62; No.800 Sqn (Code: 100/R) 30/07/62; Cat SS, HMS *Ark Royal* 30/08/62; Cat LQ, Asahan Range 18/10/62; Cat SS, HMS *Ark Royal* 91/11/62; Cat SS, HMS *Ark Royal* 30/11/62; Cat SS, Lossiemouth 15/02/63; Cat SS, HMS *Ark Royal* 4/06/63; Cat SS 10/07/63; AHU Lossiemouth 7/01/64; No.803 Sqn (Code: 148/R) 4/11/64; Cat LQ 1/12/64; Recoded (Code: 021/R) 07/65; Cat LQ, HMS *Ark Royal* 17/07/65; NASU Changi 26/04/66; No. 800B Flight (Code: 115/E) 3/06/66; AHU Lossiemouth 14/08/66; To GI Class I at AES Arbroath 3/10/66; Downgraded to GI Class II Instructional Airframe A2583 14/02/68; Downgraded to GI Class II at AES Arbroath 19/03/69; Presumed scrapped when AES Arbroath closed 31/03/71.

XD281 FF 21/08/59; AHU Lossiemouth 8/09/59; Acceptance flight 18/09/59; No.807 Sqn (Code: 190/R) 24/09/59; Hydraulic failure, controls locked and pilot ejected at 26.000ft (Lt N G Grier-Rees unhurt), Cat ZZ 10/11/59; Wreckage recovered by helicopter for AIU analysis, presumed scrapped on conclusion.

XD282 FF 16/09/59; AHU Lossiemouth 2/10/59; Acceptance flight 6/10/59; No.807 Sqn (Code: 193/R) 7/10/59; Cat SS, Lossiemouth 10/12/59; Used by Rolls-Royce pilots to test mods to Avon engine 15/12/59; Cat LQ, HMS *Ark Royal* 30/11/60; Recoded (Code: 193/C) 03/61; Cat HZ, Khormaksar 14/07/61; Recovered by MARTSU; Loaded aboard HMS *Centaur* for return to UK 20/08/61; RNAY Fleetlands for repairs and mods 14/09/61; To RNAS Lee-on-Solent 24/07/62; Demonstrated at Lee-on-Solent air show 11/08/62; AHU Lossiemouth 25/08/62; No.736 Sqn (Code: 610) 11/10/62; Ditched 2 miles E of Milltown airfield after bird strike, pilot (Sqn Ldr C D Legg unhurt) ejected, Cat ZZ 23/11/62; Wreckage recovered and to AIU at Lee-on-Solent 30/11/62; RNAY Fleetlands as scrap for disposal 8/07/63.

XD316 FF 25/09/59; AHU Lossiemouth 19/10/59; No.807 Sqn (Code: 194/R) 4/11/59; Recoded (Code: 194/C) 03/61; Cat HX, Gibraltar 17/04/61; AHU Lossiemouth 28/08/61; Cat SS 30/08/61; No.736 Sqn (Code: 612/LM) 11/12/61; Cat LQ 15/12/61; Cat SS 10/01/62; Cat LQ 23/01/62; Cat LQ 7/02/62; Cat LQ 11/05/62; Cat LQ 20/06/62; Cat LQ 4/10/62; RNAY Fleetlands for modernisation 9/10/62; RNAS Lee-on-Solent 22/07/63; Last air test at Lee-on-Solent 9/09/63; AHU Lossiemouth 27/09/63; Cat SS 18/11/63; Cat LX, RNAS Lee-on-Solent 21/11/63; RNAY Fleetlands for preparation for shipment 22/11/63; AHU Tengah for long term storage 16/01/674; NASU Sembawang for long term storage by 08/64; No.803 Sqn (Code: 015/R) 18/08/65; Aircraft pitched up on final approach, pilot (Sqn Ldr Z K Slrodski unhurt) ejected, aircraft crashed into South China Sea, Cat ZZ 28/01/66; SOC 31/01/66.

XD317 FF 6/10/59; AHU Lossiemouth 11/11/59; No.807 Sqn (Code: 197/R) 23/02/60; Recoded (Code: 197/C) 03/61; Shipped to Far East, SS *Benarty* 11/11/61; Arrived AHU Tengah; No.807 Sqn (Code: 195/C) 12/02/62; Cat LQ, Trincomalee 28/02/62; Cat LQ (mid-air collision with XD332) 18/04/62; AHU Lossiemouth 26/04/62; RNAY Fleetlands 16/05/62; RNAS Lee-on-Solent by 13/11/62; Last air test 30/11/62; No.736 Sqn 28/11/62; No.800 Sqn (Code: 113/R) 14/01/63; Cat LQ, Lossiemouth 8/04/63; Cat LQ 15/04/63; Cat LQ 24/10/63; RNAS Lee-on-Solent 27/02/64; RNAY Fleetlands for modernisation; Towed to RNAS Lee-on-Solent 7/10/65; Departed Lee-on-Solent 22/11/65, but had hydraulic failure *en route* and diverted to Boscombe Down; Returned to RNAS Lee-on-Solent 26/11/65; Departed RNAS Lee-on-Solent for RAE Bedford 6/01/66; On C(A) loan from 24/01/66; RAE Farnborough 10/03/66; RAE Bedford 1/04/66; NASU Brawdy 27/07/66; FRU Airwork 2/11/66; Coded by 10/67 (Code: 033); Recoded (Code: 833) 03/69; Cat LQ, Yeovilton ; RAE Farnborough 4/08/69; To FAA Museum, Yeovilton by road 08/69; SOC 18/09/69; Later moved from outside display to within the museum building; Extant.

XD318 FF 29/10/59; AHU Lossiemouth 5/01/60; No.807 Sqn (Code: 191/R) 14/01/60; Cat HY, HMS *Ark Royal* 6/03/60; AHU Hal Far 14/03/60; Shipped to UK; RNAS Lee-on-Solent 1/12/60; RNAY Fleetlands 2/12/60; RNAS Lee-on-Solent to Boscombe Down 23/01/61; Air tested, Boscombe Down 25/01/61; No.803 Sqn (Code: 154/V) 1/02/61; Cat LQ. Aden Protectorate 17/03/61; Cat

LQ, HMS *Victorious* 21/03/61; Cat HY, HMS *Victorious* 22/06/61; Cat SS, HMS *Victorious* 28/08/61; Cat LY, HMS *Victorious* 3/12/61; Recoded (Code: 154/H) 04/62; Cat LQ, HMS *Hermes* 13/08/62; RNAS Lee-on-Solent 13/09/62; RNAY Fleetlands for checks; RNAS Lee-on-Solent 18/11/62; RNAS Lee-on-Solent to Boscombe Down, then back 19/11/62; RNAS Lee-on-Solent to Yeovilton 20/11/62; No.803 Sqn (Code 154/H); RNAS Lee-on-Solent 24/10/63; Stored in Test Flight hangar, RNAS Lee-on-Solent 29/11/63; RNAY Fleetlands for modernisation 15/07/64; Recoded (Code: 152/R) ; RNAS Lee-on-Solent to AHU Lossiemouth 30/03/65; No.803 Sqn (Code: 152/R) 3/05/65; Recoded (Code: 025/R) 07/65; Aircraft ditched after one wave off and one bolt followed by engine failure on third attempt; pilot (Lt M J Williams) ejected safely, Cat ZZ 31/12/65; Wreckage to NASU Sembawang.

XD319 FF 16/10/59; AHU Lossiemouth 27/11/59; No.807 Sqn (Code: 192/R) 4/12/59; Cat LQ, Garvie Island 10/02/60; Cat LQ, HMS *Ark Royal* 26/04/60; AHU Lossiemouth 14/01/61; No.807 Sqn (Code: 192/C) 10/03/61; Cat LQ, HMS *Centaur* 8/07/61; Cat SS, HMS *Centaur* 30/10/61; Missed wires, failed to gain height and ditched ahead of HMS *Centaur*, pilot Sqn Ldr A D Alsop) unhurt, Cat ZZ 7/03/62.

XD320 FF 11/11/59; AHU Lossiemouth 15/12/59; No.807 Sqn (Code: 195/R) 15/01/60; HMS *Ark Royal* to RNAS Yeovilton 20/12/60; AHU Lossiemouth 22/12/60; RNAY Fleetlands 19/06/61; Air tested, RNAS Lee-on-Solent 23/08/61; Departed RNAS Lee-on-Solent 26/08/61; AHU Lossiemouth 28/08/61; No.807 Sqn (Code: 193/C) 30/08/61; AHU Tengah 31/12/62; No.800 Sqn (Code: 110/R) 12/07/62; Cat SS, HMS *Ark Royal* 8/08/62; Cat HY, HMS *Ark Royal* 7/05/63; No.803 Sqn (Code: 148/H) 26/02/63; No.800 Sqn; Cat SS, Lossiemouth 30/01/64; Recoded (Code: 148/R) during 1964; Cat LY 19/05/64; Cat LQ 1/09/64; RNAS Lee-on-Solent 16/10/64; To RNAY Fleetlands for modernisation; Towed back to RNAS Lee-on-Solent 7/01/66; Prepared for shipment by MARSTU 18/02/66; Shipped to Far East 02/66; NASU Changi 30/03/66; No.803 Sqn (Code: 015/R) 12/04/66; AHU Lossiemouth 1/10/66; NASU Brawdy 3/10/66; Awaiting disposal 19/11/69; SOC, scrapped NASU Brawdy 05/70.

XD321 FF 26/11/59; AHU Lossiemouth 25/01/60; No.807 Sqn (Code: 196/R) 30/01/60; Damaged 16/09/60; AHU Lossiemouth 10/03/61; RNAY Fleetlands 18/05/61 to 15/06/61; Air tested from RNAS Lee-on-Solent to Boscombe Down 20/06/61; Air tested, Boscombe Down 23/06/61; No.807 Sqn (Code: 194/C) 26/08/61, Cat SS, Lossiemouth 27/09/61; AHU Tengah 31/01/62; No.800 Sqn (Code: 104/R) 12/07/62; Cat SS 18/09/62; Cat HC, HMS *Ark Royal* 13/11/62; RNAY Fleetlands by 4/02/63; AHU Lossiemouth 13/02/63; No.800 Sqn 13/02/63; Damaged, HMS *Ark Royal* 28/05/62; Cat LQ, HMS *Ark Royal* 30/05/63; RNAS Lee-on-Solent 3/02/64 and on to RNAY Fleetlands for modernisation; Departed RNAS Lee-on-Solent 5/01/65; Returned to RNAS Lee-on-Solent 7/04/65; Departed RNAS Lee-on-Solent for AHU Lossiemouth 17/05/66; No.800B Flight (Code: 113/E) 11/06/65; Cat LQ 21/06/65; Recoded (Code: 116/E) 07/65; Cat LQ, HMS *Eagle* 3/09/65; Cat LQ, HMS *Eagle* 10/05/65; Cat LY, HMS *Eagle* 10/01/66; Cat SS, Changi 24/02/66; Cat LX, Changi 3/03/66; NASU Changi for repairs 3/03/66; No.803 Sqn (Code: 142/R) 12/04/66; NASU Changi 27/04/66; No.800B Flight (Code: 116/E) 23/05/66; Fuel leak, diverted to Butterworth 15/07/66; Brawdy 14/08/66; NASU Brawdy 11/10/66; Placed in open storage awaiting disposal 19/11/69; SOC and RSP 30/01/70; Scrapped by 05/70.

XD322 FF 15/12/59; AHU Lossiemouth 6/01/60; No.807 Sqn (Code: 190/R) 26/02/60; Cat LY, HMS *Ark Royal* 6/04/60; RNAS Lee-on-Solent 14/04/60; RNAY Fleetlands 25/04/60; Flown Lee-on-Solent to Boscombe Down 17/06/60; Air tested Boscombe Down 20/06/60; Via Yeovilton and North Front to No.807 Sqn (Code: 190/R) 2/07/60, Cat SS, HMS *Ark Royal* 5/12/60; No.800 Sqn (Code: 106/R) 20/03/61, Cat SS, Lossiemouth 28/07/61; Cat LQ 1/09/61; Cat SS, HMS *Ark Royal* 22/11/61; Cat LQ, diverted to Butterworth 9/04/62; Cat SS, HMS Ark royal 29/05/62; Cat SS, HMS *Ark Royal* 18/06/62; Cat SS, HMS *Ark Royal* 13/07/62; Cat SS HMS *Ark Royal* 11/09/62; Recoded (Code: 112/R) 11/62; Cat SS, Lossiemouth 11/01/63; Cat SS 20/02/63; Recoded (Code: 107/R) 04/63; Cat LQ 9/04/63; AHU Lossiemouth 24/04/63; Recoded by late 1963 (Code: 109/R); VA South Marston for modernisation 22/05/63; AHU Lossiemouth 14/07/64; To C(A) at A&AEE Boscombe Down 15/09/64; AHU Lossiemouth 6/10/64; No.803 Sqn (Code: 147/R) 15/01/65; Recoded (Code: 020/R) 07/65; Cat LX, diverted to Changi 27/01/66; NASU Brawdy 1/10/66; Station Flight, RNAS Brawdy 3/10/66; NASU Brawdy 28/02/67; RNAS Lee-on-Solent 9/03/67; RNAY Fleetlands 15/03/67; Lightered to HMS *Eagle* for deck trails 22/03/67; RNAS Lee-on-Solent 11/07/67; Departed to NASU Brawdy 27/07/67; Engine fire during test 1/08/68; FRU Airwork 11/12/68; Coded (Code: 839) 03/69; Flown to Southend Airport 2/12/70; By road

to P&EE Shoeburyness 21/12/70; Disposed out of service to RAE Farnborough 19/01/71; Used for trials at P&EE from 08/73 to 09/81; Fuselage remains scrapped at Shoeburyness by Mayer & Perry 04/91.

XD323 FF 18/01/60; AHU Lossiemouth 23/02/60; No.804 Sqn (Code: 162/H) 29/02/60, Cat HX, Garvie Island 28/03/60; Cat LQ, Lossiemouth 1/06/60; Cat SS, HMS *Hermes* 13/04/61; Cat SS 5/05/61; Cat LQ, HMS *Hermes* 8/07/61; No.800 Sqn (Code: 105/R) 13/09/61; Cat SS, HMS *Ark Royal* 13/08/62; Cat LQ 20/09/62; Cat SS, Lossiemouth 9/01/63; Cat SS, Lossiemouth 22/01/63; Cat LX, Lossiemouth 5/02/63; VA South Marston for modernisation 14/03/63; AHU Lossiemouth 6/04/64; No.803 Sqn (Code: 157/R) 14/12/64; Cat SS, HMS *Ark Royal* 16/03/65; Recoded (Code: 032/R) 07/65; Cat LQ, HMS *Ark Royal* 9/12/65; Cat SS 21/12/65; Cat SS 22/12/65; Cat HY, Changi 18/04/66; Was to be returned to RNAY Fleetlands, but not taken up; NASU Changi RSP; SOC 6/06/66; Wreckage was at NASU Sembawang 1966/7.

XD324 Tested 4-10/02/60; AHU Lossiemouth 29/02/60; No.804 Sqn (Code: 161/H) 29/02/60; Cat SS, Lossiemouth 21/06/60; Cat LX, Lossiemouth 18/11/60; Cat LQ, HMS *Hermes* 20/02/61; Cat SS, HMS *Hermes* 23/02/61; Cat SS, HMS *Hermes* 27/02/61; Cat SS, HMS *Hermes* 17/03/61; AHU Lossiemouth 18/04/61; No.804 Sqn (Code: 161/H) 28/04/61; Cat SS, Lossiemouth 11/05/61; No.800 Sqn (Code: 110/R) 13/09/61; Cat SS, Tarhuna Range 4/01/62; Cat LX, Luqa 7/01/62; Cat LQ, Tain Ranges 13/02/62; Cat LC, Garvie Island Range 27/02/62, Cat LX, HMS *Ark Royal* 7/06/62; Cat SS, HMS *Ark Royal* 14/08/62; Cat SS, HMS *Ark Royal* 2/10/62, Cat SS, HMS *Eagle* 8/11/62; Cat SS, HMS *Ark Royal* 31/01/63; Cat SS, Yeovilton 20/02/63; RNAS Lee-on-Solent 20/02/63; Towed to RNAY Fleetlands for modernisation 19/07/63; Departed RNAS Lee-on-Solent to AHU Lossiemouth 9/10/64; No.803 Sqn (Code: 158/R) 19/01/65; Cat SS, HMS *Ark Royal* 2/02/65; Cat LQ, Tain Range 9/02/65; Cat LQ 7/04/65; Cat SS 26/05/65; Recoded (Code: 033/R) 07/65; Cat LX, Labuan 18/10/65; Cat LQ, Lossiemouth 29/09/66; RNAS Lee-on-Solent 14/10/66; GI Class I 23/08/66; Downgraded to GI Class II Instruction Airframe A2590 27/02/68; To MARSTU by 20/07/70; By road to RNAY Fleetlands 21/09/70; P&EE Shoeburyness 23/09/70; Transferred to MoD(Air) and Dowty-Rotol for MRCA fuel system development work in sections 17/05/71, 8/06/71 & 23/08/71; Returned to P&EE Shoeburyness 8-14/01/75; Last noted P&EE 08/82 presumed scrapped.

XD325 Tested 14-15/03/60; To C(A) charge AHU Lossiemouth 11/05/60; No.804 Sqn (Code: 165/H) 18/05/60, Cat SS, Lossiemouth 1/06/60; Cat LQ, Hal Far 3/08/60; Cat LX, HMS *Hermes* 26/08/60, Cat LQ, HMS *Hermes* 20/01/61; Cat LX 17/05/61; AHU Lossiemouth 28/04/61; No.804 Sqn (Code: 165/H) 12/05/61; Cat LQ, HMS *Victorious* 28/07/61; No.800 Sqn (Code: 109/R) 15/09/61; Cat SS, HMS *Ark Royal* 22/11/61; Cat LQ, Tain Range 15/02/62; Cat LQ, West Freugh 22/02/62; Cat LQ, Lossiemouth 23/02/62; Cat SS, Lossiemouth 9/01/63; Cat SS 8/04/633; Cat LQ, Tain Range 18/04/63; AHU Lossiemouth 30/04/63; RNAS Lee-on-Solent 7/05/63; Towed to RNAY Fleetlands 7/06/63; Lightered to HMS *Victorious* in Portsmouth Harbour 1/07/63; Lightered back to RNAY Fleetlands for modernisation 8/08/63; RNAS Lee-on-Solent to AHU Lossiemouth 6/10/64; No.803 Sqn (Code: 151/R) 8/02/65; Cat LQ 30/03/65; Cat LQ 5/04/65; Cat LQ, Lossiemouth 12/04/65; Cat LY 28/06/65; Recoded (Code: 024/R) 07/65; NASU Changi 22/09/65; No.803 Sqn (Code: 024/R) 3/11/65; Cat HY, HMS *Ark Royal* 7/03/66; NASU Changi and RSP 21/04/66; SOC 27/04/66; Wreckage to NASU Sembawang by 01/67.

XD326 Production test flights 15/03/60-20/04/60; AHU Lossiemouth 2/05/60; No.804 Sqn (Code: 163/H) 9/05/60; Cat SS, Garvie Island Range 1/06/60; Cat SS, HMS *Hermes* 19/02/61; AHU Lossiemouth 19/04/61; No.804 Sqn (Code: 163/H) 8/05/61; Cat LQ 25/05/61; No.800 Sqn (Code: 111/R) 13/09/61; Cat LQ, USAF Wheelus, Tripoli 13/12/61; Cat LQ, HMS *Hermes* 19/03/62; Cat LQ, HMS *Hermes* 25/04/62; Cat LQ, Kai Tak 29/05/62; Cat LQ, HMS *Hermes* 25/08/62; Cat SS, Lossiemouth 4/02/63; Cat LX 11/06/63; Aircraft struck sea during low level attack of splash target, almost level astern of HMS *Ark Royal*, pilot (Lt A G MacFie) killed, Cat ZZ 31/07/63.

XD327 Allocated to VA, South Marston 30/03/60; Test flights 10-24/05/60; To C(A) charge at VA, South Marston 2/06/60; A&AEE Boscombe Down for bombing trials in El Adem 8/06/60; VA South Marston 28/07/60; AHU Lossiemouth 13/09/60; Collected by No.804 Sqn and delivered to Malta 21/11/60; AHU Hal Far 23/11/60; No.804 Sqn 5/12/60; No.803 Sqn (Code: 148/V) 16/03/61; Cat SS, HMS *Victorious* 3/05/61; Damaged, HMS *Victorious* 10/09/61; Recoded (Code: 148/H) 04/62; Cat SS, HMS *Victorious* 15/11/61; Cat SS 7/03/63; RNAS Lee-on-Solent 20/09/63; RNAY Fleetlands for modernisation (beginning 18/07/63); RNAS Lee-on-Solent to AHU Lossiemouth 25/02/65;

RNAS Lee-on-Solent for preparation for shipment 7/04/65; Cat LQ, AHU Changi 16/06/65; No.803 Sqn (Code: 031/R) 27/09/65; Cat SS 29/01/66; NASU Brawdy 3/10/66; Airwork FRU 6/04/67; Withdrawn from use 14/06/68 and used for spares; By road to RNAY Fleetlands 4/09/68; SOC and sold as scrap 7/01/69.

XD328 Production test flights 27/05/60-11/07/60; AHU Lossiemouth 13/07/60; No.803 Sqn (Code: 153/V) 26/07/60; AHU Lossiemouth 3/10/60; No.803 Sqn (Code: 153/V) 13/10/60; Cat SS, HMS *Victorious* 22/11/60; Hit by XD271 on deck, HMS *Victorious* 28/08/61; Cat SS, HMS *Victorious* 29/08/61; Tail hit XD244 during deck moves, HMS *Victorious* 27/03/62; Cat LQ, HMS *Hermes* 27/09/62; RNAS Lee-on-Solent 10/62; RNAY Fleetlands for modernisation 8/11/62; AHU Lossiemouth 1/01/64; No.803 Sqn (Code: 144/R) 6/08/64; Cat LQ 18/03/65; Cat LQ 2/04/65; Cat SS, Lossiemouth 11/06/65; Recoded (Code: 015/R) 07/65; Cat LQ 9/08/65; Cat HY, HMS *Ark Royal* 30/08/65; NASU Sembawang 16/09/65; RNAY Fleetlands 15/11/65; Stripped for spares 23/06/66; SOC & RSP 26/07/66; Hulk in scrap compound by 25/08/66.

XD329 Production test flights 27/06/60-6/07/60; AHU Lossiemouth 15/07/60; No.803 Sqn (Code: 154/V) 25/07/60; During Exercise Decex off Aden, a/c struggled to gain height after launch with 1000lb bombs and drop tanks fitted, pilot (Lt J W H Purvis) unable to maintain control, ejected (unhurt) at low level, Cat ZZ 9/12/60.

XD330 Production test flights 13/07/60-12/08/60; AHU Lossiemouth 16/08/60; No.803 Sqn (Code: 148/V) 19/10/60; Struck by Sea Vixen while on HMS *Victorious* 25/01/61; MARSTU Lee-on-Solent 8/02/61; By road to VA South Marston 15/02/61; Test flown 30/03/61; RNAY Fleetlands via RNAS Lee-on-Solent 12/04/61; No.807 Sqn (Code: 190/C) 18/04/61; Cat SS, HMS *Centaur* 30/10/61; Cat SS 11/12/61; AHU Tengah 21/02/62; No.800 Sqn (Code: 103/R) 23/10/62; No.803 Sqn (Code: 159/R) 26/02/64; RNAS Lee-on-Solent 3/07/64 and onward to RNAY Fleetlands for modernisation; Towed to RNAS Lee-on-Solent 1/09/65; Handed over to MARSTU for preparation for shipment 26/10/65; Shipped to Far East, arrived NASU Changi 4/11/65; No.803 Sqn (Code: 034/R) 20/01/66; NASU Changi 06/66; Returned to UK; NASU Brawdy 1/10/66; RSP 17/11/69; SOC 20/01/70; Scrapped at Brawdy 05/70.

XD331 Production test flights 17/08/60-31/08/60; AHU Lossiemouth 16/09/60; No.803 Sqn (Code: 145/V) 18/10/60; FOD damage to engine, HMS *Victorious* 3/11/60; Cat SS, Parhuna Range 21/11/60; Cat LQ 2/12/60; Cat LQ, HMS *Victorious* 24/01/61; Cat SS, HMS *Victorious* 7/03/61; Cat SS, RAF Tengah 8/04/61; Cat LY, HMS *Victorious* 25/11/61; Recoded (Code: 145/H) 04/62; Cat LQ 22/06/62; Cat SS, Hal Far 26/06/62; During Exercise Rip Tide II suffered fuel starvation, glided over escort HMS *Scarborough*, pilot (Lt Cdr B Wilson slightly hurt) ejected, a/c crashed into sea Cat ZZ 13/08/62; SOC 14/08/63.

XD332 Production test flights 15/09/60-21/09/60; AHU Lossiemouth 4/11/60; No.804 Sqn (No code?) 21/11/60; To Far East in HMS *Hermes* 6/12/60; AHU Tengah 30/12/60; No.807 Sqn (Code: 194/C) 8/02/62; Cat SS, Tengah 9/02/62; Cat LQ, struck XD317 in formation flypast, 18/04/62; AHU Lossiemouth 26/04/62; *en-route* to RNAS Lee-on-Solent diverted to RAF Thorney Island 24/05/62; RNAS Lee-on-Solent 25/05/62 and on to RNAY Fleetlands; RNAS Lee-on-Solent to Boscombe Down 8/12/62; Possibly returned to RNAS Lee-on-Solent 19/12/62(?); Departed RNAS Lee-on-Solent 21/12/62; No.736 Sqn (Code: 612) 11/01/63; RNAS Lee-on-Solent 5/06/63; RNAY Fleetlands 21/06/63; RNAS Lee-on-Solent to No.736 Sqn 10/07/63; Cat SS, RAE Bedford 11/12/63; Cat LQ 10/02/64; Cat SS 24/02/64; Cat LQ 28/02/64; Cat SS 2/06/64; Cat LQ 5/06/64; Heavy landing checks 13/10/64; Cat SS 5/02/65; Cat LQ 11/03/65; No.764B Sqn (Code: 616) 26/03/65; Cat LQ 17/06/65; Cat LQ 17/06/65; Cat SS 6/08/65; NASU Brawdy for temporary use by Test Pilots' course 24/11/65; RNAS Lee-on-Solent 17/02/66 and on to RNAY Fleetlands for modernisation; HMS *Hermes* for deck handling training 24/05/66; Lightered to MARSTU Lee-on-Solent for open storage 31/07/66; To GI Class II Instruction Airframe A2574 at SAH Culdrose 6/10/67; Downgraded to GI Class III 5/10/71; Towed to Cornwall Aeronautical Park, Helston 6/07/76 and repainted as 612 of No.736 Sqn; Repainted as 194/C by 09/91; By road to Southampton Hall of Aviation 10/03/99; Currently Solent Sky Exhibition, Southampton

XD333 Production test flight 22/12/60; AHU Lossiemouth 10/01/61; No.803 Sqn (Code: 147/V) 18/01/61; Cat LQ 18/04/61; Recoded (Code: 147/H) 04/62; Cat SS, HMS *Hermes* 28/05/63; Cat LQ, HMS *Hermes* 11/05/63; RNAS Lee-on-Solent 18/12/63; on to RNAY Fleetlands for modernisation after 31/01/64; Towed back to RNAS Lee-on-Solent 31/03/65; RNAS Lee-on-Solent to AHU Lossiemouth 30/04/65; Shipped to Far East; No.803 Sqn (Code: 023/R) 11/05/65; Cat SS 7/03/66; Cat SS, HMS *Ark Royal* 9/08/66; Cat LY, Lossiemouth 20/09/66; NASU Brawdy 3/10/66; Airwork FRU 3/11/67; Returned to NASU Brawdy 24/11/67;

Airwork FRU (Code: 837) 26/06/68; RAE Farnborough 20/01/71; Flown to Southend Airport 20/01/71; By road to P&EE Shoeburyness 15/02/71; SOC by RN 26/01/71; Used for trials at P&EE and gone by 12/89.

XD334 to XD357 - Cancelled

Key

A&AEE	Aeroplane and Armament Experimental Establishment, Boscombe Down (Wiltshire)
AES	Air Engineering/Electronics School
AHU	Aircraft Holdling Unit (retitled NASU c7/66)
AIU	Accident Investigation Unit
ARS	Aircraft Repair Section
AWC	Awaiting Collection
AWRE	Atomic Weapons Research Establishment
Cat HC	Heavy damage, repairable by ship or station but requiring contractors working party
Cat HX	Heavy damage, repairable by ship or station
Cat HY	Heavy damage, not repairable by ship or station
Cat LC	Light damage, repairable by ship or station but requiring contractor's working party
Cat LQ	Light damage, repairable by squadron resources
Cat LX	Light damage, repairable by ship or station
Cat LY	Light damage, not repairable by ship or station
Cat SS	No damage to aircraft
Cat ZZ	Lost, unrepairable or beyond economical repair
C(A)	Controller (Air) – ex CS(A) from 5/54
CHAG	Chain Arresting Gear
CS(A)	Controller of Supplies (Air)
DTD	Director of Technical Development
EMC	Electromagnetic Compatibility
ERU	Ejector Release Unit
ETPS	Empire Test Pilots School
FOD	Foreign Object Damage
FRU	Fleet Requirements Unit
GI	Ground Instruction (Ground Instructional Airframe)
LABS	Low Altitude Bombing System
MARU	Mobile Aircraft Repair Unit
MARTSU	Mobile Aircraft Repair, Transport and Salvage Unit
MRCA	Multi-Role Combat Aircraft (Tornado)
MTPS	Maintenance Test Pilot School
MoA	Ministry of Aviation
MoD	Ministry of Defence
NAD	Naval Air Department (RAE Farnborough and later RAE Bedford)
NAMDU	Naval Aircraft Maintenance Development Unit
NARIU	Naval Air Radio Installation Unit
NASU	Naval Aircrft Support Unit (ex AHU)
P&EE	Proof and Experimental Establishment (Shoeburyness, Essex)
RAE	Royal Aircraft Establishment (various locations)
RDU	Receipt & Despatch Unit
RNAY	Royal Naval Aircraft Yard
RN	Royal Navy
RSP	Reduced to spares & produce
SAH	School of Aircraft Handling
SOC	Struck off charge
SFS	Solf for scrap
U/c	Undercarriage
UHF	Ultra High Frequency
VA	Vickers-Armstrong Ltd
WOC	Written off charge